THE
HOUSING
OUTLOOK

THE HOUSING OUTLOOK

1980-1990

William C. Apgar, Jr.
H. James Brown
George Masnick
John Pitkin

116674

Library of Congress Cataloging in Publication Data
Main entry under title:

The Housing outlook, 1980–1990.

   Bibliography: p.
   Includes index.
   1. Housing forecasting--United States. 2. Housing
development--United States. I. Apgar, William C.
HD7293.H7 1985   338.4'769083'0973   85–16738
ISBN 0-03-005832-5 (alk. paper)

Published and Distributed by the
Praeger Publishers Division
(ISBN Prefix 0-275)
of Greenwood Press, Inc.,
Westport, Connecticut

HD
7293
·H7
1985

Published in 1985 by Praeger Publishers
CBS Educational and Professional Publishing, a Division of CBS Inc.
521 Fifth Avenue, New York, NY 10175 USA

© 1985 by Praeger Publishers

Printed in the United States of America on acid-free paper

INTERNATIONAL OFFICES

Orders from outside the United States should be sent to the appropriate address listed below. Orders
from areas not listed below should be placed through CBS International Publishing, 383 Madison Ave.,
New York, NY 10175 USA

Australia, New Zealand
Holt Saunders, Pty. Ltd., 9 Waltham St., Artarmon, N.S.W. 2064, Sydney, Australia

Canada
Holt, Rinehart & Winston of Canada, 55 Horner Ave., Toronto, Ontario, Canada M8Z 4X6

Europe, the Middle East, & Africa
Holt Saunders, Ltd., 1 St. Anne's Road, Eastbourne, East Sussex, England BN21 3UN

Japan
Holt Saunders, Ltd., Ichibancho Central Building, 22-1 Ichibancho, 3rd Floor, Chiyodaku, Tokyo, Japan

Hong Kong, Southeast Asia
Holt Saunders Asia, Ltd., 10 Fl, Intercontinental Plaza, 94 Granville Road, Tsim Sha Tsui East,
Kowloon, Hong Kong

**Manuscript submissions should be sent to the Editorial Director, Praeger Publishers, 521 Fifth
Avenue, New York, NY 10175 USA**

ACKNOWLEDGEMENTS

This report is part of an ongoing research program supported by the generosity of the Policy Advisory Board (PAB), a group of senior executives from more than twenty-five housing and housing-related companies. David Kresge, former director of the Joint Center, worked with the PAB to develop the research program on housing, demographics, and regional economics. The authors would especially like to thank Phil Clay, former Associated Director of the Joint Center, for his efforts in developing the initial research agenda that formed the basis of this study.

Preparation of this volume involved numerous staff and researchers at the Joint Center, but several deserve special mention. Jan Lent coordinated preparation of manuscript during the initial stages of the research. Manuscript editing was divided between Marcia Fernald, who was responsible for major reshaping of early drafts, and Carol Chin, who edited the final manuscript and gently nudged the authors to supply all the missing details needed to produce the final book.

The final manuscript incorporates many helpful suggestions mady by participants in the Joint Center's Housing Seminar. In particular, the authors would like to thank Professors John R. Meyer of Harvard University and Robert M. Solow of the Massachusetts Institute of Technology, senior Faculty Advisors to the Joint Center. Meyer and Solow, along with Professors John F. Kain and William Alonso of Harvard and Bernard Frieden of MIT, reviewed and provided the authors with extensive comments on an initial draft of the book. The intellectual support and guidance provided by such distinguished scholars is one of the central advantages of conducting research at the Joint Center for Housing Studies.

CONTENTS

LIST OF TABLES

LIST OF FIGURES

1

INTRODUCTION

This volume is the third in a Joint Center series on the future of housing market activity in the United States. These reports are a product of a tripartite partnership between the housing industry, government, and the university, reflecting the Joint Center's concern about the future of the housing industry and the well-being of housing consumers. The purpose of the series is to help establish benchmarks for evaluating national housing performance, to suggest goals for public policy, and to provide a base of information for both public- and private-sector decisions affecting housing. Each report analyzes trends in national and regional household growth and housing construction activity to produce a ten-year forecast of housing activity.

The research findings have important implications for the housing industry. Most current discussion is about the changing character of housing finance, yet changes in the pattern of use of the existing housing inventory and in demographic trends have equally pronounced (but largely overlooked) results. For homebuilders and producers of building materials, the message is obvious: More extensive use of the existing inventory and slowdown of household growth mean that new housing starts in the 1980s will average only about 1.6 million units per year, far below the level achieved in the 1960s and 1970s. Moreover, further declines in production are expected in the 1990s, as the baby bust generation moves into the family formation ages.

For realtors and financial intermediaries, the decline of housing activity means diminishing housing sales. As the baby boom ages, the mobility of households will lessen. In addition, many current owners faced with high housing costs may forego trading up to a new unit in favor of upgrading the unit they already own.

Counteracting the reduced business opportunities in new housing will be an increase in investment activity in the existing inventory, including expenditures in maintenance, repair, alteration, and conversion of the current housing stock. Thus, these trends have important consequences for all those involved in the housing sector: consumers, home-builders, realtors, building material suppliers, and government institutions. Public- and private-sector decision makers must therefore improve their understanding of basic demographic, economic, technological, political, and social factors that shape housing supply-and-demand patterns.

Previous Studies

The 1973 report, <u>America's Housing Needs: 1970-1980</u>, forecasted 23 million units of new construction over the decade.[1] This was substantially below the conventional wisdom of the time that had expected a national "housing production goal" of about 26 million, but was close to the actual construction of 21 million.[2] While the forecast was accurate on the overall level of activity, it did less well in forecasting some of the components. The report underestimated the demand for housing that would be generated by new household formation, assuming about 14 million new households, compared to the actual growth of nearly 17 million. In contrast, the report overstated the need to replace housing lost or removed from the inventory. The forecast of 7 million units of replacement was substantially higher than the actual net loss of about 2.5 million. Part of this overestimate resulted from failing to anticipate the substantial increase in the amount of rehabilitation and conversion that would occur over the decade.

The 1973 report proved accurate in forecasting the distribution of U.S. housing activity, both regionally and by metropolitan and non-metropolitan areas. A major proportion of housing activity occurred in the South and only about one-third in the East and North Central regions.[3] Further, the growth in non-metropolitan parts of the country was a significant departure from historical trends.

The study also attempted to measure the extent of inadequate housing in 1970. The authors broadened earlier
conceptions of social housing needs by arguing that housing
deprivation took several different forms: physically inadequate housing units, overcrowding, excessive cost burden,
and inadequate neighborhood conditions. Applying the first
three measures of deprivation to census data, the report
estimated that in 1960, 15.3 million of the total 73.4
million households, or roughly 21 percent, were housing-
deprived, and that this figure had dropped to about 13.1
million in 1970. Most of this deprivation was due to
physical inadequacy (about 7 million households), approximately 1 million households were overcrowded, and another 5
million were paying excessive rents relative to their
incomes.

The second report in this series, The Nation's Housing:
1975-1985, was published in 1977 and continued the work of
forecasting housing activity and measuring the extent of
housing deprivation.[4] This report did not have any new
comprehensive census data, but it profited from experience
during the early part of the decade to produce a much more
extensive analysis of the determinants of household formation. Recognizing the rapid growth of households over the
first part of the 1970s, the authors established that the
earlier forecasts would underestimate household formation
and predicted a higher rate of household growth. At the
same time, they realized that the rapid rate of household
growth was not likely to continue indefinitely, and expected household formation to crest and stabilize. The
1977 report also benefited from more accurate and complete
migration estimates done at the Joint Center. The previous
study had made use of migration forecasts prepared elsewhere, which had been generally accurate, but had under-
stated the migration to the South and West.

The Nation's Housing also considered some of the important issues surrounding affordability of housing and particularly of homeownership. The authors analyzed some of
the trends in housing costs and anticipated problems of
affordability over the last half of the 1970s and the first
half of the 1980s.

The study also continued the analysis of the extent and
pattern of housing deprivation and found that 16.8 million
households were inadequately housed. The dimensions of
housing deprivation included neighborhood inadequacy, a
measure made possible for the first time by a new data

source, the <u>Annual Housing Survey</u>. Households suffering
from high rent burdens and inadequate neighborhoods were
located overwhelmingly in the metropolitan areas, those
living in physically inadequate housing largely in rural
areas. As excessive rent began to replace slum housing as
the dominant form of housing deprivation, the authors
concluded that housing policies should increasingly include
income assistance to the poor. They noted, however, that
housing policies should be tailored to the conditions of
different areas.

Data Sources

Since the last report, the Center has produced its own
forecast of population, <u>The Changing Population of States
and Regions</u> (1982).[5] This forecast, which differs from
those of the Bureau of the Census, provides new insight
into the effect of regional distribution of population on
housing activity. Also, the release of the 1980 Census of
Population and Housing permitted a much more extensive look
at the factors affecting household formation in the 1970s
and a continuation of the Center's analysis of housing consumption based on cohort trends. The census data also made
possible a much more comprehensive analysis of changes in
the housing inventory over the decade, especially changes
in the reuse of the existing stock through rehabilitation
and conversion and in the rate of removal of existing stock
from the usable inventory. Finally, better and more complete data have permitted an extension of the analysis of
trends in housing affordability, first presented in the
1977 report. The present report updates that work and
extends the analysis to include the effects of both taxes
and inflation on the cost of homeownership.

The work for this report was started in 1982 with the
first available data, incorporating new information as it
was released by the Census Bureau. Unfortunately, some of
the data was not released according to the original
timetable, and our research plan had to be modified. Fur-
thermore, some of the new data necessitated updating or re-
fining work that had already been completed. We have
attempted to include as much as possible of the updated
analysis in this volume, and have included references to
some of the more recent work in the notes. All of the
forecasts and policy discussions, however, reflect the most
recent data and analysis.

Organization of the Study

The forecast offered in this manuscript is based on analysis of the experience of the housing sector over the past decade. We present our results in two parts. In the first (Chapters 2 through 5) we describe our analysis of the major factors affecting the housing industry during the 1970s. In the second (Chapters 6 through 8) we build on that analysis of historical trends to produce our forecast for the 1980s.

Our analysis of the housing sector in the 1970s documents trends in major factors affecting housing activity: housing demand, supply responses, and housing costs. Chapters 2 and 3 examine housing demand, considering in turn changes in the rate of household formation and in housing consumption. Chapter 4 discusses the changes in the inventory over the decade, isolating the separate effects of new construction, rehabilitation and conversion, and losses on the size of the housing stock. This section also highlights regional variations in the use and preservation of the stock. The fifth chapter integrates the analyses of demand and supply by describing changes in housing prices and rents and the issues of housing affordability. These changes are analyzed for the nation as a whole and for counties based on region, urban/rural status, and rate of household growth over the decade.

The second part of the study draws on our analysis of the 1970 trends to produce the Center's forecast for the 1980s. Chapter 6 puts this forecast in perspective by reviewing the major alternative forecasts of the housing sector. Chapter 7 presents the Center's estimates of population, households, homeownership, housing stock losses, new construction, and rehabilitation and conversion both for the nation as a whole and for the nine major census divisions. The concluding chapter gives our interpretation of some of the major implications of these forecasts for housing and urban policy in the U.S.

Summary of the Results

Population and Household Growth. From the record growth of 16.8 million in the 1970s, we estimate that increases in the number of total households in the 1980s will fall to approximately 14.0 million. The number of young adults in the prime household formation ages of 20 to 34 will increase by 5 million between 1980 and 1985, and

after 1985 begin to decline as the baby-bust generation
replaces the baby-boom cohorts.   By 1985 the growth of
population aged 20 to 24 will slow sharply and by 1990 will
actually have declined by more than 1.0 million.

Demographic changes affect the housing sector not only
through population and household growth, but also through
changes in life style and housing consumption.   Young
adults have delayed marriage and couples have chosen to
have fewer children and to have them later. We expect that
young adults will continue to make these choices throughout
the remainder of the decade.   As a result the housing demand caused by the baby-boom generation starting families
will be spread out more slowly over the rest of the century. The oldest of the baby-boom group (born between 1945
and 1955), however, are reaching middle age with established families, thus strengthening the demand for tradi
tional detached single-family housing.

Changing Utilization of the Housing Inventory.   During
the 1970s the nation experienced a dramatic decline in net
housing losses.   Although demolitions continued at a high
rate in central cities of the Northeast and North Central
regions, losses decreased sharply elsewhere.   The 1970s
also witnessed a sharp growth in the number of non-new
construction additions to the housing stock.   Subdivision
of large single-family homes into two or more dwelling
units and conversion of warehouses, schools, and other nonresidential buildings into apartments and condominiums
added from 2.7 to 3.9 million units to the inventory over
the decade.   Although conversion activity is frequently
associated with older cities in the Northeast and North
Central regions of the country, non-new construction additions have contributed significantly to the growth of the
housing inventory in the central city, suburban, and rural
areas in all regions of the country.

The reduction of losses and the increase in conversions
and other non-new construction additions to the inventory
are the responses of the housing market to the rising costs
of housing capital, as well as to the changing patterns of
housing demand as average household size declines.   Further, the high quality of the country's housing stock
implies an increasing role of remodeling, repair, and reno-
vations in maintaining the existing inventory.   Over the
decade, investment in the existing inventory will account
for a growing share of the country's housing investment.

   Regional Trends.   The well-documented shift of population and new housing activity from the Northeast and
North Central regions to the South and West continued
through the 1970s.   Over two-thirds of the growth in the
housing inventory occurred in the South and West.   The
1970s also witnessed the movement of population from larger
metropolitan areas to smaller cities, towns, and rural
areas.   For the first time in 150 years, housing in rural
counties expanded more rapidly than in urban counties.
   We found no evidence from our study of the regional
trends to expect that the patterns of the 1970s will be
reversed during the 1980s.   We expect population in the
Northeast and North Central regions to increase by only one
percent over the decade and the number of households by
only seven percent.   Intra-regional shifts of population
and households will increasingly determine the demand for
new construction in these regions.   The South and West, by
contrast, are projected to grow substantially over the
decade and will continue to attract a large share of
migrants.

   Homeownership Affordability.   What has come to be
called the homeownership "affordability crisis" has its
roots in a number of complex and interrelated changes that
have occurred since 1973.   Four factors have played a major
role in raising the costs of homeownership: changes in the
mortgage market and higher interest rates resulting from
Federal Reserve Bank monetary policies, coupled with rising
federal deficits and deregulation of the savings and loan
industry; inflation in home prices and in the expectations
of future gains through appreciation; movement of the baby-
boom generation into the prime homebuying stages; and the
rising cost of complying with government regulations.
   Between 1973 and 1975, although utility costs increased
substantially,   overall   homeownership   costs   nonetheless
remained remarkably stable.   The housing market boom years
occurred in 1975-1979, when rapid increases in home prices
yielded large capital gains to homeowners.   While potential
buyers faced higher overall costs during the latter 1970s,
these higher prices did not prevent many households from
buying their own homes.
   Between 1979 and 1982, however, mortgage rates rose 60
percent while utility costs increased 30 percent faster
than inflation.   These increases, together with the high
prices resulting from the earlier boom and the lower

expected gains from subsequent housing price inflation, left potential homebuyers in 1981 and 1982 with few options. Those households that did not make the transition to homeownership, and new households that were entering the market for the first time, have recently been facing increasingly unfavorable conditions. Younger and poorer households are now less likely to own their own homes than they were five years ago. Those that have been able to purchase houses are much more likely to have selected condominiums or mobile homes than they were before. Households that were able to afford the traditional single-family detached home are more likely to have selected a smaller unit with fewer amenities.

   Housing in the 1980s. We predict a baseline of 14 million new households and 18.9 million newly constructed units of housing in the 1980s. Allowing for mobile home placements of approximately 2.9 million units, this implies 16 million units of conventional housing starts. The total predicted level of new housing is 2 million units lower than the number added in the 1970s and from 5 to 10 million units lower than the amount predicted by other forecasters. The Joint Center estimates are based on detailed analysis of demographic patterns that affect household composition and growth and of conversion and rehabilitation activities that substitute for new housing construction. Recent revisions by others have narrowed the difference in the forecasts, but these revisions have been made on an ad hoc basis because of the poor performance of the U.S. and world economies in the early part of the decade. The Joint Center forecast, based on demographic and industry trends, gives a better insight into the factors affecting future housing market activity.

                              NOTES

   1. David L. Birch et al., America's Housing Needs: 1970-1980 (Cambridge, MA: Joint Center for Urban Studies of MIT and Harvard University, 1973).

   2. The President's Committee on Urban Housing, A Decent Home (Washington, DC: U.S. Government Printing Office, 1968). The committee's "housing production goal" was not

technically a forecast, but a statement of housing needs over the decade. The distinction between a statement of needs and a forecast is that the former contains some normative judgment about the amount of housing production that is necessary to provide an adequate rate of improvement in housing conditions.

3. Throughout this study we will be referring to geographical divisions as used by the Census Bureau. They are as follows: New England (Maine, New Hampshire, Vermont, Massachusetts, Rhode Island, and Connecticut); East North Central (Ohio, Indiana, Illinois, Michigan, and Wisconsin); West North Central (Minnesota, Iowa, Missouri, North Dakota, South Dakota, Nebraska, and Kansas); East South Central (Kentucky, Tennessee, Alabama, and Mississippi); West South Central (Arizona, Louisiana, Oklahoma, and Texas); Middle Atlantic (New York, New Jersey, and Pennsylvania); South Atlantic (Delaware, Maryland, District of Columbia, Virginia, West Virginia, North Carolina, South Carolina, Georgia, and Florida); Mountain (Montana, Idaho, Wyoming, Colorado, New Mexico, Arizona, Utah, and Nevada); Pacific (Washington, Oregon, California, Arkansas, and Hawaii).

4. Bernard Frieden and Arthur Solomon, The Nation's Housing: 1975 to 1985 (Cambridge, MA: Joint Center for Urban Studies of MIT and Harvard University, 1977).

5. George Masnick and John Pitkin, The Changing Population of States and Regions (Cambridge, MA: Joint Center for Urban Studies of MIT and Harvard University, 1982).

2

HOUSEHOLD GROWTH

The 1970s witnessed an unusually rapid growth in the number of households and a marked change in household composition. Between 1970 and 1980, 16.8 million households were added to the stock, compared with net additions of about 10.6 million in each of the previous two decades. With the arrival of the baby-boom generation into the prime household formation ages, the strong growth in the number of households was entirely expected; the large swings in growth rates and in the distribution of household types, however, were not. This chapter analyzes the causes of instability in household growth over the past decade and examines regional variations in these trends.

National Trends: 1950-1980

It was clear in the late 1960s that the maturing of the baby-boom generation (cohorts born between 1945 and 1964) would mean significant growth in the number of households. What forecasters failed to anticipate was that the percentage of unmarried adults who headed their own households would also rise dramatically. In 1950, married couples headed almost 80 percent of the existing households and almost 65 percent of the new households added over the subsequent decade. Since 1960, however, the share of household growth attributable to married couples has fallen precipitously: Table 2.1 shows that by the 1970s, the

11

Table 2.1

HOUSEHOLDS BY TYPE, 1950-1980

Household Type	Number of Households				Change over Decade		
	1950	1960	1970	1980	1950-60	1960-70	1970-80
	(as percentage of total)						
Married-couple Households	77.4	74.7	69.1	60.5	63.8	41.5	27.6
Single-person Households	9.4	13.3	17.5	22.7	29.0	38.4	42.1
Other Female Household Heads	8.1	8.0	8.6	10.3	7.4	11.8	17.0
Other Male Household Heads	5.2	4.0	4.7	6.5	-0.1	8.3	13.3
	(in thousands)						
Total Households*	42,394	53,024	63,638	80,434	10,630	10,614	16,796

Figures are percentages of total.
* Total households figures in thousands.

SOURCE: Census of Population and Households, 1950-1980, various tables (Washington, DC: U.S. Government Printing Office).

decade of largest total household growth in history, married couples headed only 28 percent of new households formed, whereas single persons headed 42 percent. The number of husband-wife households thus increased only 10.5 percent over the 1970s, while the number of single-person households grew by 63.5 percent.

The 1980 distributions of household types shown in Figure 2.1 reaffirm these trends. Married couples accounted for only 60 percent of all households, and this share has declined continuously since 1950. Households headed by married couples have decreased not only in the percentage of the total households, but also in the size of the household itself. In 1980, only 50 percent of all married couples had children under the age of 18 living with them (down from 56 percent in 1970), and these families were only 30 percent of all households (compared with almost 39 percent in 1970). There are several reasons why fewer children are present in married-couple households. First, young couples are waiting longer to have children. Second, young parents are having fewer children. The freedom of choice offered by modern birthcontrol methods, together with a general shift toward less child-oriented life styles, means that women born during the mid-1950s will bear a record low number of children. For some married couples, this will mean no children at all.

The third factor contributing to the smaller married-couple households is that the parents of the baby-boom generation are increasingly in the "empty nest" stage of the life cycle. Since most empty-nest households contain no more than two adults, the longer such households continue, the more they reduce the average size of all married-couple households. It is also noteworthy that as the years before and after raising children represent an increasing share of the total life span of a married-couple household, children are present for a smaller share of that life span.

Another significant change over the decade is the substantial growth in the number of adults who have chosen to live alone. In 1970, 19.8 percent of unmarried persons over the age of 15 lived alone; by 1980, the share of unattached adults who headed single-person households rose to 24.4 percent.

Part of the increase in single-person households can be explained by the growing population in categories with a higher frequency of living alone, particularly among the elderly (Figure 2.2). In addition, there has been a steady

Figure 2.1

DISTRIBUTION OF HOUSEHOLDS BY TYPE, 1950-1980

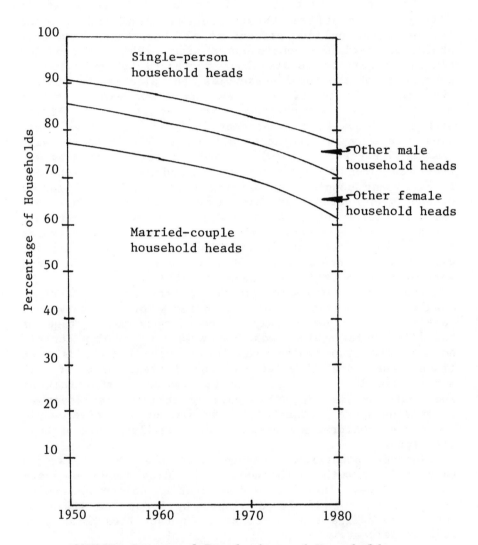

SOURCE: Census of Population and Households, 1950 to 1980, various tables (Washington, DC: U.S. Government Printing Office).

Figure 2.2

UNMARRIED INDIVIDUALS BY AGE, SEX,
AND HOUSEHOLD STATUS, 1980

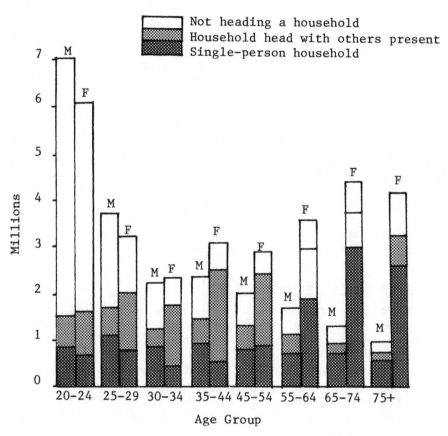

M = male; F = female.

SOURCE: U.S. Bureau of the Census, Current Population
Reports, series P-20, no. 365 (Washington, DC: U.S. Government Printing Office, 1980).

rise in the percentage of unmarried individuals who have chosen to live alone. Figure 2.3 shows the change between 1970 and 1980 in the percentage living alone by sex and marital status. For all unmarried individuals, the proportion living alone has increased from about 13 to 20 percent for men and from 22 to 30 percent for women. This increase occurs in all categories of unmarried men, while for women the change is largely due to widows living alone. More women than men fall into the widowed category, which has the highest rate of living alone, and thus, among all unmarried adults, more women live alone than men. In all other marital categories, more men live alone primarily because women are more likely to have children in their households. Never-married individuals, both men and women, are the least likely to live alone since they tend to be younger and to live with either parents or roommates.

The longer-term trend in the rates at which unmarried men and women head households is documented in Table 2.2. Before 1950, headship rates increased only among the young; after 1950, however, rates for all age groups rose. Although a slowdown appears between 1970 and 1980 in the growth of headship rates among older unmarried men, it should be noted that this group represents a very small fraction of the total unmarried population.

The Components of Household Growth

The causes of household growth can be separated into three components: the age structure factor, the migration factor, and the household formation factor.[1] The age structure factor captures the effects of simple aging of the population, as the baby-boom and baby-bust generations move into the household formation stage, and as longevity among the elderly improves. In the 1970s, the age structure factor accounted for almost 63 percent of the total increase in households.

The migration factor accounts for 17 percent of household growth for the nation as a whole. This factor is significant because of the sizable increase over the decade in the number of immigrants from abroad. It is even more important in regional analysis because population movement around the country causes geographic variation in growth rates.

The number of households formed by a given population also depends on how the population distributes itself among various family types, since this affects headship rates.

Figure 2.3

ADULTS LIVING ALONE BY SEX AND
MARITAL STATUS, 1970-1980

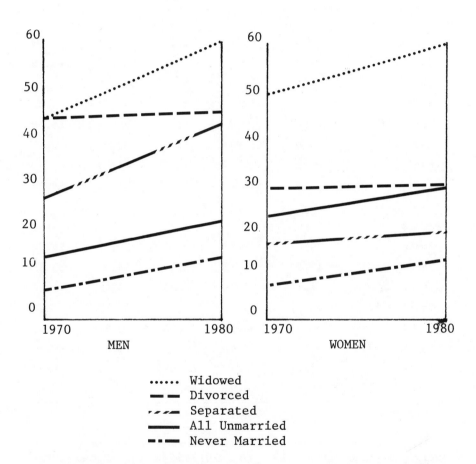

...... Widowed
— — Divorced
⸗⸗ Separated
——— All Unmarried
—·— Never Married

SOURCE: U.S. Bureau of the Census, Current Population
Reports, series P-20, nos. 212, 287, and 365 (Washington,
DC: U.S. Government Printing Office, 1970 and 1980).

Table 2.2

UNMARRIED ADULTS HEADING THEIR OWN HOUSEHOLDS, 1940-1980
(in percentages)

Age and Sex	1940	1950	1960	1970	1980
Males					
20-24	3.25*	4.17*	5.98	12.21	20.99
25-29	7.74	9.61	16.31	32.62	45.00
30-34	14.38	15.76	24.59	40.78	55.70
35-44	24.95	25.64	33.54	49.28	60.50
45-54	38.04	37.40	44.52	59.21	65.45
55-64	47.50	44.92	51.37	65.03	70.27
65-74	50.50	48.34	54.77	66.69	70.49
75+	42.49	41.36	45.81	55.50	59.74
Females					
20-24	4.27*	7.27*	12.37	20.17	26.38
25-29	11.92	17.72	30.11	49.33	55.35
30-34	24.18	29.36	42.83	60.01	70.04
35-44	43.07	43.55	54.61	67.12	77.60
45-54	55.46	54.93	61.50	71.58	78.67
55-64	55.93	55.42	62.62	73.61	80.16
65-74	52.02	52.42	60.83	72.33	79.81
75+	40.85	40.56	46.68	55.30	62.84

* Includes heads under age of 20.

SOURCE: Calculated from data contained in Census of Population, various tables, 1940 to 1970; and Census of Population and Housing, 1980, public use microdata sample, B sample, 1983 (Washington, DC: U.S. Government Printing Office).

For example, divorced females with children are more likely
to head a household than are childless divorced females.
Similarly, the number of households may differ over time or
between regions, although the total population is the same,
due to differences in headship rates. Changes in headship
rates over time are shown in Table 2.2, and regional variations are discussed in a later section. Due to data
limitations, these two effects are calculated as one
residual, the household formation factor. Nationwide,
then, this factor accounts for 20 percent of the household
growth between 1970 and 1980.

At the same time, the overall contribution of the
household formation factor combines the opposite effects of
changes in marital status and changing headship rates. The
declining percentage of individuals ever married served to
reduce the total number of households since never-married
men and women in their early 20s more often live in households with three or more adults, including parents or
roommates. However, this reduction is offset by rising
divorce rates over the decade and the tendency to live
alone immediately after divorce which help raise headship
rates and increase the number of households. Because more
of the baby-boom generation fell into the never-married
group than the divorced group, the net effect of changing
marital status on the total number of households was therefore negative.

Rising headship rates among almost all age and marital
status groups nonetheless served to increase the total
number of U.S. households over the 1970s. Since these two
opposing changes in marital status and headship rates are
combined in the household formation factor, it is important
to underscore that the gross changes are considerably
greater than the net changes show.

The Age Structure Factor

As Figure 2.4 illustrates, the number of new households
attributable to the simple aging of the population between
1970 and 1980 shows little regional variation from the
national average. The change in age structure had the
least effect in the Middle Atlantic states and the most in
the Mountain states. Thus the regional distribution of
individuals born between 1940 and 1960 (cohorts who were in
the prime household formation ages in the 1970s) remained
fairly close to the distributions of the original birth
cohorts.[2] What variation there is among regions results

Figure 2.4

COMPONENTS OF HOUSEHOLD GROWTH BY CENSUS DIVISION, 1970-1980

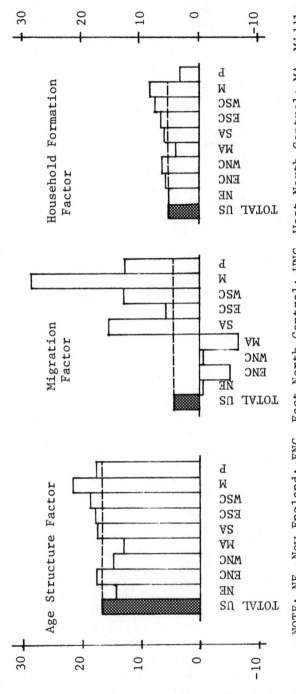

NOTE: NE, New England; ENC, East North Central; WNC, West North Central; MA, Middle Atlantic; SA, South Atlantic; ESC, East South Central; WSC, WEst South Central; M, Mountain; P, Pacific.

SOURCE: Joint Center tabulations on Census of Population and Housing, 1970 and 1980 (Washington, DC: U.S. Government Printing Office).

from differences in the magnitude of the baby boom in each region and from pre-1970 migration of children (with their parents) and young adults.

Table 2.3 shows, as measured by children ever born per woman aged 15-44 in 1960, that the baby boom was smallest in the Middle Atlantic region (1.54 children per woman) and largest in the Mountain states (1.99 children per woman). Differentials in fertility rates change the age structure of the population and affect later household growth rates when the increased young population reaches the household formation age. Thus the 24.1 percent increase in the number of children ever born per woman during the 1950s showed up in household growth in the 1970s.

During the 1960s, the total number of children ever born declined by 8.3 percent for the U.S. as a whole, a decrease that will reduce household growth in the 1980s. The major effect of the baby bust on net new household formation will not be seen until the 1990s, however, when the children born during the 1970s, at a 20.8 percent lower rate nationwide, reach young adulthood. The baby bust was somewhat more uniformly distributed across the regions than the baby boom had been, with the lowest birthrates in the Middle Atlantic and New England and the highest in the Mountain and South Central regions. Thus, the age structure factor allows us to use fertility trends to project from the existing population the size of the household-forming population 20 years into the future.

The Migration Factor

Although immigration contributed only 4.4 percent to household growth for the nation as a whole, population redistribution around the country had a much greater effect on individual regions. As Figure 2.4 illustrates, migration accounted for a substantial gain in new households in the sunbelt and a loss in the frostbelt. For the Mountain states, the migration factor induced almost as much of the increase in household growth as did the age structure and household formation factors combined. The East North Central and Middle Atlantic divisions lost over 1.4 million households, or as much as the gain in the South Atlantic region.

Not only does the migration factor vary across regions, but it also varies over time. During the 1950s, for example, the East North Central and Middle Atlantic divisions gained new households through migration; by the 1970s,

Table 2.3

CHILDREN EVER BORN PER WOMAN AGED 15–44, 1950–1980

Census Divisions	Number of Children				Rate of Change (%)		
	1950	1960	1970	1980	1950–60	1960–70	1970–80
New England	1.332	1.688	1.610	1.210	26.7	- 4.6	-24.8
East North Central	1.380	1.790	1.678	1.336	29.7	- 6.3	-20.3
West North Central	1.448	1.897	1.757	1.341	31.1	- 7.4	-23.7
Middle Atlantic	1.181	1.542	1.510	1.212	30.6	- 2.1	-19.7
South Atlantic	1.445	1.731	1.597	1.275	19.8	- 7.7	-20.2
East South Central	1.675	1.919	1.716	1.422	14.6	-10.6	-17.1
West South Central	1.619	1.932	1.733	1.448	19.3	-10.3	-16.4
Mountain	1.622	1.987	1.769	1.420	22.5	-11.0	-19.7
Pacific	1.403	1.860	1.648	1.271	28.2	-11.4	-22.9
TOTAL	1.468	1.827	1.675	1.326	24.1	- 8.3	-20.8

SOURCE: Census of Population and Households, 1950–1980, various tables (Washington, DC: U.S. Government Printing Office).

though, this trend had reversed itself. These changes suggest that assumptions about migration for sub-national areas over one or two decades can be a significant source of errors in forecasting households.

When changing numbers of households are analyzed at the state level, the degree of variability in the migration factor increases still further. Even within regions, some states gain while others lose households. In the 1970s, for example, New England as a whole experienced a modest decline of 13,000 in the total number of households. Within the region, however, New Hampshire gained 47,000 households through migration while Massachusetts lost 65,000. In the South Atlantic region, the District of Columbia lost 61,000 households due to migration (23 percent of its 1970 total), while Florida gained 1.1 million (almost 50 percent of its 1970 total). Although migration effects have generally been secondary to age structure effects in accounting for change in the total number of households, notable exceptions exist in almost every region (Table 2.4).

The Household Formation Factor

Like the age structure factor, the household formation factor did not exhibit nearly as much regional variation as the migration factor during the 1970s. Since similar trends in family formation and headship over the decade apply to all regions, the household formation factor produced a fairly uniform pattern of household growth across the country. The region that experienced the smallest average growth in households due to the household formation factor (the Pacific) was also the region that experienced the largest increase in the proportion of each age group that was never married. Because the marital status and headship components of the household formation factor are both large and of opposite sign, however, they deserve separate discussion.

Trends in Marital Status. Between 1970 and 1980, the population over the age of 15 increased by 20 percent. If marriage rates had remained at 1970 levels, this change in the population base would have caused both the never-married and the currently married segments to grow by approximately the same amount. As Table 2.5 indicates, however, the number of never-married individuals increased by 36 percent over the decade, while the number of those

Table 2.4

COMPONENTS OF CHANGE IN TOTAL NUMBER OF HOUSEHOLDS BY REGIONS AND STATES, 1970–1980

Census Division and States	Total Change		Due to Age Structure		Due to Migration		Due to Household Formation	
	Thousands	(%)	Thousands	(%)	Thousands	(%)	Thousands	(%)
New England	705	(19.3)	523	(14.3)	-13	(-0.4)	196	(5.4)
ME	92	(30.1)	43	(14.1)	26	(8.6)	23	(7.5)
NH	97	(43.0)	34	(15.1)	47	(20.6)	17	(7.3)
VT	45	(33.9)	23	(17.1)	12	(9.2)	10	(7.6)
MA	265	(15.1)	241	(13.7)	-65	(-3.7)	90	(5.1)
RI	45	(15.5)	42	(14.5)	-15	(-5.2)	18	(6.3)
CT	160	(17.1)	139	(14.9)	-18	(-1.9)	38	(4.1)
East North Central	2,258	(18.2)	2,186	(17.6)	-630	(-5.1)	701	(5.6)
OH	541	(16.4)	583	(17.7)	-229	(-6.9)	186	(5.7)
IN	324	(20.1)	291	(18.1)	-57	(-3.5)	90	(5.6)
IL	541	(15.4)	550	(15.7)	-195	(-5.6)	186	(5.3)
MI	532	(20.0)	541	(20.3)	-148	(-5.5)	138	(5.2)
WI	320	(24.0)	221	(16.6)	-1	(-0.1)	101	(7.5)
West North Central	1,036	(20.0)	751	(14.5)	-34	(-0.7)	318	(6.2)
MN	285	(24.6)	197	(17.0)	13	(1.2)	74	(6.4)
IA	157	(17.4)	122	(13.5)	-20	(-2.3)	55	(6.1)
MO	268	(17.6)	198	(13.0)	-7	(-0.4)	77	(5.1)
ND	47	(25.9)	33	(18.0)	-5	(-2.7)	19	(10.6)
SD	43	(21.1)	32	(15.6)	-7	(-3.6)	18	(9.0)
NB	97	(20.4)	66	(13.8)	-1	(-0.1)	32	(6.7)
KS	141	(19.3)	105	(14.4)	-8	(-1.1)	43	(5.9)

Census Division and States	Total Change Thousands	(%)	Due to Age Structure Thousands	(%)	Due to Migration Thousands	(%)	Due to Household Formation Thousands	(%)
East South Central	1,167	(30.0)	692	(17.8)	221	(5.7)	254	(6.5)
KY	276	(27.9)	167	(16.9)	45	(4.5)	64	(6.5)
TN	398	(32.7)	207	(17.0)	113	(9.3)	79	(6.5)
AL	303	(29.2)	194	(18.7)	41	(4.0)	68	(6.6)
MS	190	(29.6)	125	(19.5)	22	(3.4)	43	(6.7)
West South Central	2,331	(39.0)	1,117	(18.7)	776	(13.0)	439	(7.3)
AR	203	(32.8)	81	(13.1)	82	(13.2)	40	(6.5)
LA	364	(34.4)	236	(22.3)	38	(3.6)	89	(8.5)
OK	261	(30.6)	119	(14.0)	90	(10.6)	52	(6.1)
TX	1,503	(43.7)	681	(19.8)	565	(16.4)	257	(7.5)
Middle Atlantic	1,219	(10.3)	1,539	(13.0)	-794	(6.7)	474	(4.0)
NY	397	(6.7)	748	(12.6)	-580	(-9.8)	228	(3.8)
NJ	328	(14.7)	301	(13.5)	-52	(-2.3)	79	(3.5)
PA	495	(13.3)	490	(13.2)	-163	(-4.4)	168	(4.5)
South Atlantic	3,691	(39.0)	1,670	(17.6)	1,454	(15.3)	567	(6.0)
DE	42	(25.3)	33	(20.0)	2	(0.9)	7	(4.3)
MD	288	(24.5)	231	(19.6)	0	(0.0)	57	(4.9)
DC	-10	(-4.0)	43	(16.2)	-61	(-23.0)	7	(2.8)
VA	462	(33.1)	288	(20.7)	88	(6.3)	85	(6.1)
WV	138	(25.0)	79	(14.3)	20	(3.7)	39	(7.0)
NC	530	(35.0)	323	(21.3)	99	(6.5)	109	(7.2)
SC	292	(39.5)	183	(24.8)	68	(9.2)	41	(5.6)
GA	497	(36.2)	292	(21.3)	117	(8.5)	88	(6.4)
FL	1,452	(63.4)	198	(8.6)	1,121	(48.9)	133	(5.8)

Table 2.4, continued

Census Division and States	Total Change		Due to Age Structure		Due to Migration		Due to Household Formation	
	Thousands	(%)	Thousands	(%)	Thousands	(%)	Thousands	(%)
Mountain	1,470	(58.2)	540	(21.4)	720	(28.5)	209	(8.3)
MT	68	(31.0)	40	(18.2)	12	(5.5)	16	(7.3)
ID	105	(47.8)	43	(19.4)	44	(20.1)	18	(8.3)
WY	61	(58.3)	20	(19.5)	29	(28.0)	11	(10.9)
CO	366	(52.8)	143	(20.7)	162	(23.3)	61	(8.8)
NM	153	(52.8)	75	(25.8)	53	(18.3)	25	(8.7)
AZ	423	(78.2)	106	(19.7)	273	(50.6)	43	(8.0)
UT	150	(50.2)	82	(27.6)	46	(15.6)	21	(7.1)
NV	144	(89.8)	31	(19.2)	100	(62.3)	13	(8.3)
Pacific	2,920	(33.7)	1,525	(17.6)	1,111	(12.8)	283	(3.3)
WA	434	(39.2)	198	(17.9)	163	(14.7)	73	(6.6)
OR	300	(43.3)	106	(15.3)	143	(20.7)	51	(7.4)
CA	2,045	(31.0)	1,141	(17.3)	762	(11.6)	142	(2.2)
AK	52	(65.5)	28	(35.5)	13	(15.9)	11	(14.0)
HI	89	(43.4)	52	(25.4)	30	(14.8)	7	(3.3)
TOTAL	16,796	(26.4)	10,543	(16.6)	2,810	(4.4)	3,442	(5.4)

NOTE: State numbers may not add up to regional totals because of rounding.

SOURCE: Joint Center calculations using 1970 and 1980 published census data by age and sex (Census of Population and Housing: General Characteristics) and 1970 Public Use Sample (1-in-100) (Washington, DC: U.S. Government Printing Office).

currently married increased by only 13 percent. This shift occurred because fewer people chose to marry and those who married later. Those regions of the country that lost population through migration had the lowest growth in both never- and currentlymarried individuals. Those areas that gained migrants, especially the South Atlantic, Mountain, and Pacific regions, experienced a greater-than-average increase in both the number and proportion of the population remaining single.

In combination, then, for regions receiving migrants, the changing age distribution and shift in marriage patterns meant a growth in the never-married population at rates far above the national average. While the number of never-married adults rose 36 percent over the decade in the nation as a whole, this group grew by 45 percent in the South Atlantic region, 64 percent in the Mountain region, and 52 percent in the Pacific region. Even the three regions with the least change in the percentage remaining single (the more rural and more traditional West North Central, East South Central, and West South Central states) still experienced significant overall growth in the size of the never-married group due to the shift in the age distribution of the population base.

The largest percentage increase in any marital category was among the formerly married: those who were divorced, legally separated, or had an absent spouse. For the United States as a whole, the number of the formerly married rose 44 percent. The frostbelt regions showed the largest increase and the sunbelt regions (with the exception of the Mountain states) the smallest.

The number of widowed individuals, the last marital status category described in Table 2.5, also rose over the 1970s. The sharp decline in mortality rates resulted in a modest overall increased in the widowed population. Those regions with a large number of elderly migrants showed the largest gains in life expectancy. These gains can probably be attributed to the fact that the most likely elderly to migrate are the healthy married couples. It is possible, though, that retirement migration itself may have beneficial effects on health and longevity because of improvements in climate and psychological well-being.

As interesting as trends in marital status are in their own right, the principal focus here is on how they affect the number of households being formed. The decline in both marriage and fertility rates would be expected to result in fewer households, yet Figure 2.4 and Table 2.5 show an

Table 2.5

COMPONENTS OF CHANGE IN POPULATION OVER 15 BY MARITAL STATUS AND REGION, 1970-1980

Census Division	Total Population 1970	Total Population 1980	Change 1970-80	Due to Change in Population Base (%)	Due to Change in Marital Status (%)	Total Change (%)
			Never-married Population (both sexes)			
NE	2,222,265	2,899,532	677,267	14.5	16.0	30.5
ENC	6,615,145	8,418,434	1,803,289	11.9	15.4	27.3
WNC	2,696,064	3,341,294	645,230	13.2	10.7	23.9
MA	6,735,519	8,447,223	1,711,704	8.4	17.0	25.4
SA	4,979,843	7,243,881	2,264,038	24.9	20.6	45.5
ESC	1,982,007	2,641,165	659,158	19.7	13.6	33.3
WSC	2,938,581	4,205,280	1,266,699	29.3	13.8	43.1
M	1,309,074	2,144,947	835,873	42.2	21.7	63.9
P	4,441,186	6,773,492	2,332,306	26.7	25.8	52.5
TOTAL	33,919,684	46,115,248	12,195,564	18.5	17.5	36.0
			Currently Married Population (both sexes)			
NE	5,074,387	5,351,008	276,621	13.9	-8.4	5.5
ENC	17,774,842	18,511,867	767,025	12.3	-8.0	4.3
WNC	7,335,134	7,996,714	661,580	14.3	-5.3	9.0
MA	16,186,880	15,781,687	-405,193	5.5	-8.0	-2.5
SA	13,390,585	16,616,290	3,225,705	32.3	-8.2	24.1
ESC	5,608,533	6,648,578	1,040,045	23.6	-5.1	18.5
WSC	8,495,191	10,828,704	2,333,513	32.5	-5.0	27.5
M	3,635,972	5,139,719	1,503,747	50.7	-9.3	41.4
P	11,579,426	13,783,594	2,203,168	30.4	-11.4	19.0
TOTAL	89,050,950	100,657,161	11,606,211	20.9	-7.9	13.0

Census Division	Total Population 1970	Total Population 1980	Change 1970-80	Due to Change in Population Base (%)	Due to Change in Marital Status (%)	Total Change (%)
		Divorced, Separated, Spouse Absent Population (both sexes)				
NE	508,865	733,659	224,794	14.7	29.5	44.2
ENC	1,826,703	2,630,863	804,160	12.5	31.5	44.0
WNC	637,596	895,998	258,402	14.6	25.9	40.5
MA	1,786,681	2,301,376	514,695	6.3	22.5	28.8
SA	1,798,419	2,657,898	859,479	31.4	16.4	47.8
ESC	668,069	906,555	238,482	23.6	12.1	35.7
WSC	1,068,808	1,562,530	493,722	32.7	13.5	46.2
M	419,221	765,194	345,973	52.3	30.2	82.5
P	1,786,849	2,662,511	875,662	30.3	18.7	49.0
TOTAL	10,501,211	15,116,584	4,615,373	22.3	21.7	44.0
		Widowed Population (both sexes)				
NE	722,969	770,562	47,593	16.3	-9.7	6.6
ENC	2,219,525	2,410,705	191,180	15.7	-7.1	8.6
WNC	977,385	1,048,970	71,585	14.5	-7.7	7.3
MA	2,414,820	2,495,385	80,565	12.5	-9.2	3.3
SA	1,813,474	2,338,837	525,363	40.5	-11.5	29.0
ESC	799,038	940,925	141,887	26.5	-8.7	17.8
WSC	1,096,580	1,314,835	218,255	30.9	-11.0	19.9
M	371,265	488,180	116,915	48.8	-17.3	31.5
P	1,323,284	1,577,772	254,488	31.3	-12.1	19.2
TOTAL	11,738,340	13,386,171	1,647,831	23.2	-9.6	13.6

Regional figures may not add up to totals due to rounding.

See Figure 2.4 for abbreviations.

SOURCE: Census of Population and Housing: General Characteristics, 1970 and 1980, and Census of Population and Housing: Public Use Sample (1-in-100), 1970 (Washington, DC: U.S. Government Printing Office).

increase in households attributable to the household formation factor. Even without data on regional headship rates,
it is clear that this increase must be due to a rapid rise
in headship rates. In addition, these data imply that
considerable difference in headship rates exists between
the frostbelt and sunbelt regions, and that the influence
of this variation is in the opposite direction from the
regional variation in marital status. To yield the small
regional variation in the combined household formation
factor depicted in Figure 2.4, the frostbelt states must
have experienced higher gains in headship rates to compen
sate for the greater growth in unmarried population.

     Trends in Headship Rates. The data presented in Table
2.6 divide the household population into four marital
status categories: never-married, married couples, widows,
and all those previously married except widows.[3] The
proportion of people heading a household increased in all
of the unmarried groups. By 1980, the headship rate for
previously married individuals appears to have stabilized
near 80 percent, and for widows between 80 and 90 percent.
Headship rates among the never-married population are still
well below those characteristic of other unattached adults.
It should be noted that because the statistics in Table 2.6
are based on the population living in households, they are
not a good measure of headship rates among all unmarried
adults below age 25, and particularly those below age 20,
because the proportions of these age groups in the household and non-household populations (such as college dormitories) have varied considerably over time. Sample survey
data are insufficient to examine similar trends in headship
on a regional basis, and as stated earlier, delay in the
release of 1980 census data has forestalled our efforts to
make regional comparisons.

Implications for Forecasting

     During the 1970s, the most significant impact on the
growth of households nationally was that of the aging of
the baby-boom cohorts, who began to form households in
large numbers. The number and type of households formed
were also substantially affected by such changes in life
style as delayed marriage, increased divorce, and the
increased tendency of all age groups to form separate
households. Both life style and age structure factors
acted fairly uniformly across the country; on a regional

Table 2.6

HEADSHIP RATES BY AGE AND MARITAL STATUS, 1960-1980

Age Group	1960	1970	1975	1980	1960	1970	1975	1980
	Currently Married Couples				Never-married Men and Women			
15-19	.8356	.8690	.8975	.8964	.0064	.0103	.0169	.0174
20-24	.9467	.9616	.9701	.9610	.0885	.1592	.1948	.2116
25-29	.9760	.9860	.9839	.9836	.1954	.3397	.4369	.4425
30-34	.9841	.9925	.9936	.9893	.2662	.3931	.5003	.5726
35-39	.9884	.9946	.9931	.9952	.3194	.4152	.5310	.5789
40-44	.9908	.9958	.9956	.9948	.3657	.4468	.5297	.5831
45-49	.9902	.9954	.9939	.9964	.4293	.4964	.5492	.5735
50-54	.9905	.9947	.9957	.9935	.4834	.5316	.5372	.6004
55-59	.9892	.9928	.9917	.9953	.5101	.5970	.5772	.5920
60-64	.9832	.9909	.9925	.9910	.5606	.6257	.6267	.6490
65-69	.9772	.9873	.9886	.9873	.6015	.6501	.7088	.7251
70-74	.9695	.9847	.9841	.9906	.5913	.6559	.6890	.7735
	Widows				Previously Married Men & Women			
15-19	.2953	.3395	--	.4355	.0939	.1408	.2197	.2201
20-24	.4894	.7132	.6798	.8140	.2763	.3873	.5389	.5476
25-29	.7137	.8136	.9417	.8616	.4556	.5961	.7067	.6865
30-34	.7996	.8486	.8954	.9216	.5554	.7015	.8062	.7700
35-39	.7917	.8942	.9021	.9184	.6309	.7313	.8266	.8358
40-44	.8134	.8936	.9280	.9042	.6543	.7531	.8534	.8362
45-49	.8089	.8837	.9295	.8823	.6758	.7652	.8221	.8526
50-54	.7919	.8602	.9085	.8691	.6804	.7521	.8061	.8406
55-59	.7576	.8411	.8769	.9061	.6803	.7619	.8309	.8463
60-64	.7120	.8168	.8765	.8590	.6774	.7609	.8147	.8404
65-69	.7019	.7978	.8550	.8689	.6575	.7594	.8541	.8418
70-74	.6651	.7711	.8303	.8630	.6521	.7537	.8079	.8676

SOURCE: Joint Center tabulations on Census of Population and Housing Public Use Sample (1-in-100), 1960 and 1970; and on Annual Housing Survey National Sample, 1975 and 1980 (Washington, DC: U.S. Government Printing Office).

level, migration becomes the most significant factor in
accounting for variations in household growth.

The implications for forecasting are complex. The age
structure factor, which is the easiest to estimate since
the age distribution of the existing population is known,
is the least important for forecasting housing activity on
a regional level. The migration factor is the most criti-
cal element for regional household forecasts and is the
most difficult to predict. Finally, the trends in marital
status and headship rates must be carefully watched,
although they do not vary substantially by region, because
they can have a pronounced effect on the demand for housing. In the next chapter, we describe our method for
analyzing how variations in family and household types
influence the demand for housing.

NOTES

1. This line of analysis was suggested in a paper by
William Alonso, "The Demographic Factor in Housing for the
Balance of this Century," North American Housing Markets
into the Twenty-First Century, edited by Michael A. Goldberg and George W. Gerr (Cambridge, MA: Ballinger, 1983).
To accomplish this, we first calculate an expected population by age and sex for each region for 1980 under the
assumption that net migration for each state was zero for
the entire 1970-1980 decade. That is, the only way that we
allowed the population to change in each state was through
mortality of the existing population in 1970. This hypothetical 1980 population was then distributed by marital
status according to the 1970 state distribution. Finally,
1970 headship rates by state, age, sex, and marital status
were applied in order to calculate the hypothetical number
of households that would be present in 1980 if everything
were held constant at 1970 levels except the aging of the
population. The difference between the actual 1970 number
of households and this hypothetical figure is the change
attributed to the age structure factor.

Next, the actual 1980 population by age and sex in each
state was used along with the 1970 marital status distributions and headship rates to calculate another hypothetical
number of households. This time, the difference between
this new hypothetical number and the hypothetical number

calculated under the zero migration assumption is the change due to the migration factor. Finally, by adding together the changes due to the age structure and migration factors and subtracting this from total actual changes in number and type of households in each state between 1970 and 1980, the result is the change not explained by age structure or migration. This residual change is due to the combined effects of changing marital status and changing headship rates, or what we have called the household formation factor.

Other approaches have combined the age structure and migration factors into a "population change" factor, and then partitioned the population change effect into a "population growth" factor (simple increase in the number of people over the age of 15) and a "population composition" factor (especially, shift in the age distribution). According to this methodology, both the population growth and population composition factors contain the influences both of the simple aging of the population already in place and of migration. Our aim is to separate the components of demographic change that are largely independent of economic factors (age structure effects) from those that depend more closely on the economic climate operating during the period of change (migration effects and household formation effects).

2. Here we are not referring to individuals who are still residing in their region of birth, but to the ratio of the size of the cohort in residence relative to the size of the cohort of birth. To a large extent, those who move out of each region are replaced by others who are the same age.

3. Because Table 2.6 mixes both census (1960 and 1970) and Annual Housing Survey data (1975 and 1980) (the former based upon an enumeration of the entire resident population and the latter based on a sample of the household population only) the calculation includes only that portion of the census data representing persons living in households. Limiting data to the household population only when calculating headship rates has the effect of raising the rates because numerators are unaffected but denominators are smaller.

3

HOUSING CONSUMPTION

In order to forecast accurately housing sector activity it is necessary to determine not only the number of households, but also the nature of the demand for housing by these households. This demand depends on the type and characteristics of the households as well as on household income and the cost of housing. Historically, certain patterns of housing demand have emerged. Most people leave their parents' households when in their early twenties and begin by renting their units. They become homeowners in their late twenties and early thirties and then move up into larger and more expensive houses during their late thirties and early forties. In some cases, as homeowners become elderly, they give up their large houses and become renters once again.

To analyze these patterns of housing consumption we use a technique called <u>cohort analysis</u>, which follows the housing consumption over time of birth cohorts (groups born in a particular period) as they age. The conventional cross-sectional method compares the situation of different birth cohorts at a given time to infer the pattern of change in housing consumption over the life cycle. Because cohort analysis takes into account how a given population group adjusts its housing consumption over time, this method indicates the future effects of a cohort's current housing consumption, which cross-sectional analysis cannot do. It is important to trace such linkages over time, especially when significant differences exist in the current housing consumption of cohorts of different ages.

The Cohort Approach

With few exceptions, available census and survey data do not allow the tracking of individuals' housing consumption over time. Lacking such longitudinal data on "housing careers," this analysis links the 1960 and 1970 Census Public Use Sample with the 1975 and 1980 Annual Housing Survey (National) data tapes to construct cohort trajectories.[1] Respondents are assigned to a particular five-year cohort by age. It should be noted, however, that this synthetic cohort method measures aggregate net rather than gross changes in housing consumption. For example, the percentage of married couples aged 40-45 in 1970 who were homeowners might be higher than the percentage when the same group was aged 30-35 in 1960, a difference that results from more renter households becoming owners than the number of owner households becoming renters.

Early life transitions such as leaving the parental home, completing education, settling into a job, getting married, and raising children are major factors that affect housing consumption. Net changes are therefore higher among younger groups. For example, five percent of the cohort born between 1956 and 1960 headed renter households when they were aged 15-19 in 1975; five years later, the number had grown to 26 percent of the same cohort. (Since this is a net increase, it represents the difference between those who became heads of renter households for the first time and those who had been renter heads at ages 15-19 and became homeowners or members of other households at ages 20-24.)

Later net transitions in housing occupancy (caused by departure of grown children, retirement, and widowhood) usually occur over longer intervals. The proportion of the cohort aged 30-34 in 1975 heading renter households, for example, decreased by less than three percentage points over the next five years, compared with a 21 point increase for the cohort that was 15 years younger. Over three-quarters of the household heads over age 64 in 1970 had not moved for more than five years, over five times the proportion of 25-29-year-olds who had not moved.

The following discussion of housing consumption transitions between 1960 and 1980 focuses on the segment of each cohort that headed households, subdivided by types of housing units, but not by marital status. Some of the transitions and intercohort differences in headship rates or other aspects of housing consumption may therefore be attributed to differences in marital status or shifts in patterns within marital status categories. In instances where changes in marital status appear to have contributed significantly to net differences in housing consumption, this fact is noted.

Cohort Trends in Housing Consumption: 1960-1980

Rather than attempting to discuss all 17 cohorts that have passed through any part of the age span 15 to 85 since 1960, this analysis focuses on the housing careers of four representative cohorts. Table 3.1 shows the progress of all age groups through the housing consumption cycle, with special attention to the selected baby-boom, depression, World War I, and late 1890s cohorts.

Born between 1946 and 1950, the early baby-boom cohort entered the housing market for the first time during the late 1960s. By 1980, when this cohort was 30-34 years of age, 55 percent headed their own households and 64 percent of households owned their house or apartment.

The depression cohort, born 15 years earlier, was aged 45-49 in 1980. Having entered the housing market during the boom of the 1950s, this cohort traded up over the last 20 years at an unprecedented rate: both total homeownership and ownership of larger houses increased substantially.

In sharp contrast to the depression cohort, the World War I cohort, born between 1916 and 1920, made much more modest gains in housing between 1960 and 1980. Their rate of homeownership increased only slightly, mostly in owner- ship of small- and medium-sized houses.

The cohort born in the late 1890s who were in their early sixties in 1960 adjusted down their housing consump- tion over the two decades to fit their new circumstances. Headship rates rose by one-fifth, reflecting the increasing number of widows and widowers, while homeownership rates declined, especially for ownership of larger units.

Between 1960 and 1980, the four representative birth cohorts each lived through one stage of the typical housing career--getting started, getting ahead, settling in, and adjusting down. The sections below describe the housing consumption patterns in each of these stages.

Table 3.1

COHORT PROGRESSION THROUGH THE HOUSING CYCLE, 1960-1980

Cohort Born	I: Getting Started		II: Getting Ahead			III: Settling In				IV: Holding On			
	20-24	25-29	30-34	35-39	40-44	45-49	50-54	55-59	60-64	65-69	70-74	75-79	80-84
1956-60	1980												
1951-55	1975	1980											
1946-50/Baby Boom Cohort	1970	1975	1980										
1941-45		1970	1975	1980									
1936-40	1960		1970	1975	1980								
1931-35/Depression Cohort		1960		1970	1975	1980							
1926-30			1960		1970	1975	1980						
1921-25				1960		1970	1975	1980					
1916-20/World War I Cohort					1960		1970	1975	1980				
1911-15						1960		1970	1975	1980			
1906-10							1960		1970	1975	1980		
1901-05								1960		1970	1975	1980	
1896-00/Late Nineties Cohort									1960		1970	1975	1980
1891-96										1960		1970	1975
1886-90											1960		1970
1881-85												1960	
1876-80													1960

NOTE: Years listed are those in which the center of the cohort passes through the midpoint of the age group.

SOURCE: Compiled by the authors.

Getting Started: The Baby-boom Cohort. The first baby-boom cohort (born 1946-1950) was just getting established in the housing market between 1960 and 1980. Because the data on this young cohort is so sketchy prior to 1970, we pick up their housing consumption story then. Table 3.2 shows that in 1970 almost 38 percent of the 15 million members of this cohort (then aged 20-24) were maintaining separate households. While 43 percent of the cohort were never married, 16 percent of households were headed by a never-married adult. Between 1970 and 1975, the proportions that headed households rose by about 15 percent. After age 30 (1975 to 1980), the headship rate increased much more slowly, rising only another three points to 55 percent.

Never-married and formerly married individuals headed a larger proportion of the baby-boom cohort's households even though the share of the cohort that was married rose from 50 percent in 1970 to 72 percent in 1975. The increase in households headed by single adults resulted from much higher headship rates among the never-married population in their twenties (an increase from 16 to 44 percent) plus a substantial rise in the number of separated or divorced adults. In 1970, formerly married individuals made up 7 percent of the baby-boom cohort's population and headed just over 7 percent of its households; by 1975, these shares had risen to 10 and 14 percent, respectively, and by 1980, to 14 and 20 percent.

Table 3.2 also displays the housing consumption patterns of this cohort. In 1970, almost three-quarters of this first babyboom cohort were renters. The households were fairly evenly distributed among rental unit types: large multi-family (five or more units), small multi-family (two to four units), and single-family dwellings. As the cohort matured, it rapidly moved into homeownership. By 1975, almost half the households headed by this cohort at ages 25-29 were homeowners; most owned medium-sized units (five to six rooms in one- to four-family structures).

After age 30, nearly two million more households became owners and the number of renters decreased by over one-fifth. As a result, almost two-thirds of the cohort's households were homeowners in 1980, with nearly one-quarter owning houses with seven or more rooms.

Compared with earlier cohorts at the same age, the baby-boom generation is more likely to head a household, be divorced, and rent an apartment, and less likely to be married and own a home. It is important to understand such

Table 3.2

MARITAL STATUS AND HOUSING CONSUMPTION
OF THE FIRST BABY-BOOM COHORT, 1960–1980

Marital Status and Housing Consumption	1960 (10–14)	1970 (20–24)	1975 (25–29)	1980 (30–34)
Marital Status				
Population (in thousands)	--	15,125	16,913	17,526
Married (%)	--	50.1	71.9	73.5
Never Married (%)	--	43.0	17.9	12.2
Formerly Married (%)	--	6.9	10.2	14.3
Headship Rate (%)	--	37.8	52.1	55.1
Household Heads (in thousands)	--	5,719	8,816	9,654
Married (%)	--	76.7	71.0	67.2
Never Married (%)	--	16.0	15.0	12.7
Formerly Married (%)	--	7.3	13.9	20.1
Housing Consumption				
Homeowners (%)	--	27.6	48.2	66.3
1–4 Rooms, 1–4 Families	--	4.4	4.3	4.1
5–6 Rooms, 1–4 Families	--	13.5	26.3	31.0
7+ Rooms, 1–4 Families	--	3.6	12.4	24.0
Apartment	--	0.3	0.5	1.0
Mobile	--	5.9	4.7	3.3
Renters (%)	--	72.4	51.8	36.7
1 Family	--	23.5	17.4	12.9
2–4 Families	--	22.6	13.8	9.3
Apartment	--	24.6	19.4	13.5
Mobile	--	1.7	1.2	1.0

NOTE: Population here includes only those living in households. Thus over time the cohort is "joined" by individuals
coming from college dormitories and military housing.

SOURCE: Joint Center tabulations from 1970 Census Public
Use Sample, and 1975 and 1980 Annual Housing Survey tapes
(Washington, DC: U.S. Government Printing Office).

differences among cohorts, both in initial situations and in later adjustments, in order to predict household forma tion behavior and housing consumption.

Getting Ahead: The Depression Cohort.   In 1960, the depression cohort resembled most cohorts aged 25 to 29: 86 percent of the cohort had been married, and married couples headed 88 percent of all households (Table 3.3).   Half of the members of the cohort headed households, and half of these owned their own homes.   Of the 2.47 million home- owners, over 60 percent occupied medium-sized houses, 20 percent smaller houses, and 14 percent larger houses.   A majority of the 2.55 million renter households also lived in single-family houses; 26 percent occupied two- to four- family units, and 19 percent resided in apartments.   Only two percent of the never-married and nine percent of those who were formerly married owned their own homes.

During the 1960s the depression cohort, then in their thirties, improved their housing consumption substantially. The number of homeowners increased by over 50 percent and nearly 70 percent of all households owned their homes by the end of the decade.   In 1970, at ages 35-39, this cohort included 3.92 million homeowners, 1.44 million of whom had houses with seven or more rooms.   Ownership of small houses, on the other hand, dropped from 10 percent of the cohort's households in 1960 to only five percent in 1970. Fully 77 percent of the married couples had bought their own homes; since couples still accounted for more than four-fifths of all households formed by the depression cohort, the proportion of renters thus fell by 37 percent. Rental occupancy declined significantly in small multiple- family buildings and only slightly in large multiple-family buildings.

The increase in housing consumption among the depres- sion cohort is related to family characteristics. Women in this cohort had the highest completed fertility and lowest rate of childlessness of all the groups of baby-boom parents. By ages 25-29, 68 percent of the cohort's married women already had two or more children; some 12 percent of these larger families occupied houses with at least seven rooms, about twice the rate for families with fewer chil- dren. By 1970, the share of married women in the depres- sion cohort who had borne two or more children had risen to 84 percent, and 36 percent of these families had moved up to large houses.   Only 18 percent of the married couples

Table 3.3

MARITAL STATUS AND HOUSING CONSUMPTION
OF THE DEPRESSION COHORT, 1960-1980

Marital Status and Housing Consumption	1960 (10-14)	1970 (20-24)	1975 (25-29)	1980 (30-34)
Marital Status				
Population (in thousands)	10,577	10,833	11,275	11,403
Married (%)	79.6	83.5	83.2	79.5
Never Married (%)	14.0	6.5	4.8	4.5
Formerly Married (%)	6.4	10.0	12.0	16.1
Headship Rate (%)	47.5	52.1	53.8	54.8
Household Heads (in thousands)	5,023	5,642	6,064	6,336
Married (%)	87.9	80.5	76.0	70.7
Never Married (%)	5.8	5.2	4.8	4.8
Formerly Married (%)	76.4	14.4	19.2	24.5
Housing Consumption	49.2	69.6	74.3	76.6
Homeowners (%)				
1-4 Rooms, 1-4 Families	10.0	5.1	4.5	5.2
5-6 Rooms, 1-4 Families	30.2	36.9	37.5	37.0
7+ Rooms, 1-4 Families	7.0	25.6	28.9	30.2
Apartment	0.2	0.4	0.6	1.1
Mobile	1.8	1.7	2.8	3.0
Renters (%)	50.8	30.4	25.7	23.4
1 Family	27.4	14.2	11.3	8.9
2-4 Families	13.3	7.7	6.0	5.1
Apartment	9.9	8.3	8.1	8.9
Mobile	0.2	0.2	0.3	0.5

NOTE: Population here includes only those living in households. Thus over time the cohort is "joined" by individuals
coming from college dormitories and military housing.

SOURCE: Joint Center tabulations from 1970 Census Public
Use Sample, and 1975 and 1980 Annual Housing Survey tapes
(Washington, DC: U.S. Government Printing Office).

with smaller families owned houses with seven or more
rooms.

Over the 1970s, the depression cohort continued to
improve their housing situation, albeit more slowly. The
headship rate rose slightly, homeownership increased, and
rental occupancy declined. In 1980, 77 percent of the 6.1
million households and 88 percent of the 4.5 million
married couples (now in their late forties) owned their own
homes. Ownership of large houses among this group had
increased from 1.4 million to 1.8 million.

Rental of units in one- to four-family structures
continued to decline over the decade. Since 1970, however,
the proportion of the depression cohort renting apartments
in larger buildings has increased, due to both the greater
availability of such units in the stock and higher rates of
divorce, separation, and widowhood. Formerly married
individuals accounted for 14 percent of the cohort's households in 1970, but 25 percent in 1980; at the same time,
the share of households headed by married couples fell from
81 to 71 percent. It should be noted that a high proportion of the formerly married in their thirties and forties
are only recently divorced (or widowed). The normal tendency is for one of the partners to keep the house that the
couple lived in while married or at least to maintain the
same standard of living in a new unit. Housing consumption
patterns among the formerly married are thus related to
those of the currently married. The significant increase
in home equity and real income between 1960 and 1980 may
have contributed to the ability of formerly married individuals to keep their houses.

Increases in housing consumption slowed markedly as the
depression cohort reached their early forties. Homeownership and the occupancy of large houses increased only half
as rapidly between 1975 and 1980 as in the preceding five
years. Indeed, all of the birth cohorts passing through
the ages of 40-64 between 1960 and 1980 display a pattern
of increasing rates of headship, homeownership, and consumption of large houses. Due to attrition in the size of
the cohort through mortality, however, the number of households, homeowners, and owners of large houses remained
roughly stable for these cohorts.

Settling In: The World War I Cohort. During the 1960s
and 1970s, the housing consumption pattern of the World War
I cohort (born 1916 to 1920) was typical of those in the
settling-in phase. As shown in Table 3.4, in 1960 when

Table 3.4

MARITAL STATUS AND HOUSING CONSUMPTION
OF THE WORLD WAR I COHORT, 1960-1980

Marital Status and Housing Consumption	1960 (10-14)	1970 (20-24)	1975 (25-29)	1980 (30-34)
Marital Status				
Population (in thousands)	11,394	10,891	10,354	9,910
Married (%)	84.8	80.1	77.5	72.9
Never Married (%)	6.1	5.3	4.7	4.9
Formerly Married (%)	9.1	14.6	17.8	22.3
Headship Rate (%)	50.6	53.4	55.0	56.5
Household Heads (in thousands)	5,766	5,817	5,697	5,595
Married (%)	83.1	73.1	67.5	60.9
Never Married (%)	4.4	5.3	4.9	5.6
Formerly Married (%)	12.5	21.6	27.6	33.5
Housing Consumption				
Homeowners (%)	67.9	73.2	76.0	76.7
1-4 Rooms, 1-4 Families	10.5	10.6	9.8	10.3
5-6 Rooms, 1-4 Families	38.8	41.0	43.3	42.7
7+ Rooms, 1-4 Families	17.4	18.5	18.8	18.3
Apartment	0.4	0.8	1.0	1.5
Mobile	0.9	2.3	3.0	3.8
Renters (%)	32.1	26.8	24.0	23.3
1 Family	16.5	10.1	9.3	7.7
2-4 Families	8.2	7.9	6.1	5.9
Apartment	7.4	8.6	8.2	9.1
Mobile	0.0	0.2	0.4	0.6

NOTE: Population here includes only those living in households. Thus over time the cohort is "joined" by individuals
coming from college dormitories and military housing.

SOURCE: Joint Center tabulations from 1970 Census Public
Use Sample, and 1975 and 1980 Annual Housing Survey tapes
(Washington, DC: U.S. Government Printing Office).

they were aged 40-44, 85 percent of the cohort was married and 83 percent of the households were married couples. Over half of the cohort headed their own households; of the 5.8 million units they occupied, slightly more than two-thirds were owned. While a majority of the homeowners occupied medium-sized houses, over one-fourth owned larger houses, and fewer than one in six had houses of less than five rooms. Half of the renters lived in single-family houses, while less than one-fourth lived in units in two-to four-family structures.

In 1970, when members of this cohort were aged 50-54, the total number of households formed by the cohort was almost the same as in 1960. But, since half a million of this age group had died, this implies a five percent increase in the rate of household headship. Over the decade, there was a net increase of 300,000 owner households, mostly in medium- and large-sized homes. Some growth also occurred in the number of mobile homes owned and apartments rented by members of the cohort, but the number of small houses owned remained virtually constant.

Between 1970 and 1980, both household headship and homeownership rates continued to grow. By 1980, when they were aged 60-64, 77 percent of the households in this cohort owned their residences. In 1960, 73 percent of the married couples in the cohort were homeowners; by 1980, this proportion had risen to 88 percent. Those who were either never married or formerly married made even greater gains in homeownership over the period--increases of 25 and 20 percent, respectively. Headship rates among individuals of these marital statuses also rose between 1960 and 1980. It should be noted, however, that never-married and divorced or separated households comprised only five and seven percent, respectively, of the cohort in 1970; such large net shifts in homeownership and headship rates for these subgroups therefore represent only modest changes for the cohort as a whole.

This cohort was well housed in 1980. Over 60 percent of households owned their own homes of five or more rooms. Since they were in their early sixties and their children were likely to have moved out, one would suspect that they had very adequate space. Occupancy of single-family rental units decreased much more slowly in the 1970s than in the previous decade. But the cohort's rental of units in two-to four-family structures--which had remained unchanged between 1960 and 1970--dropped substantially.

The housing pattern of the World War I cohort between 1960 and 1980 is characteristic of this stage of life. Up to their early fifties many are still buying their first home or trading up to larger houses; from their early fifties through age 65, however, the cohort accomplishes a net stabilization of its housing situation.

Adjusting Down: The Late 1890s Cohort. When a cohort ages beyond 60, the consequences of mortality (which include both decline in total population and increases in the number and percentage of widows) dominate its housing consumption decisions. Widowhood typically reduces the surviving spouse's income and ability to cope with the maintenance and operation of a separate housing unit. The final phase of the housing cycle can therefore be described as one of adjusting down from earlier levels. It is also the normal time for retirement, with a consequent freedom from constraints on location but also some reduction of income. At this age, people more frequently suffer infirmities and are more generally eligible for subsidized housing than younger individuals.

The late 1890s cohort was in the final stage of its life course between 1960 and 1980. As Table 3.5 indicates, deaths reduced the cohort's total size by 24 percent (from 6.94 to 5.30 million) and its married population by 1.97 millon over the 1960s. During the following decade, the total elderly population declined by 52 percent, and married individuals declined by 69 percent.

The net result of these deaths is to increase the number of formerly married individuals, a group with relatively high headship rates. As noted in Chapter 2, the shift into marital status categories with higher headship rates (as distinguished from changes in headship rates within marital status groups) is termed the marital status factor. This factor, rather than higher rates of headship within particular marital classes, accounts for most of the increase in household headship among elderly cohorts.

Between 1960 and 1980, members of the late 1890s cohort made significant changes in their housing choices. At ages 80-84 in 1980, 18 percent of the cohort's households resided in apartment buildings with five or more units, up from 11 percent in 1960. While some of this increase is no doubt due to the simple fact that age, living alone, and infirmity frequently made it harder for the elderly to keep up houses, it is also true that the building boom of the

Table 3.5

MARITAL STATUS AND HOUSING CONSUMPTION
OF THE LATE 1890S COHORT, 1960–1980

Marital Status and Housing Consumption	1960 (10-14)	1970 (20-24)	1975 (25-29)	1980 (30-34)
Marital Status				
Population (in thousands)	6,944	5,292	3,967	2,565
Married (%)	69.6	54.0	47.1	34.3
Never Married (%)	6.8	6.8	6.5	4.9
Formerly Married (%)	23.7	39.3	46.4	60.8
Headship Rate (%)	50.8	55.9	59.6	62.5
Household Heads (in thousands)	3,532	2,964	2,363	1,603
Married (%)	60.0	38.3	25.3	18.6
Never Married (%)	7.4	7.9	7.1	5.8
Formerly Married (%)	32.6	53.7	66.6	75.6
Housing Consumption				
Homeowners (%)	68.7	65.9	65.3	62.7
1-4 Rooms, 1-4 Families	15.9	17.3	16.0	14.7
5-6 Rooms, 1-4 Families	35.4	33.6	33.7	31.7
7+ Rooms, 1-4 Families	15.6	11.3	11.0	10.7
Apartment	0.8	1.3	1.5	2.1
Mobile	1.0	2.5	3.1	3.4
Renters (%)	31.3	34.1	34.7	37.3
1 Family	12.0	9.5	9.7	10.7
2-4 Families	8.5	10.1	9.4	9.8
Apartment	10.7	14.2	15.2	16.0
Mobile	0.1	0.3	0.4	0.8

NOTE: Population here includes only those living in households. Thus over time the cohort is "joined" by individuals coming from college dormitories and military housing.

SOURCE: Joint Center tabulations from 1970 Census Public Use Sample, and 1975 and 1980 Annual Housing Survey tapes (Washington, DC: U.S. Government Printing Office).

1970s and the availability of federal housing subsidies made apartment living more attractive.

Members of the late 1890s cohort increased their occupancy of mobile homes from one percent in 1960 to over three percent 20 years later. This trend is due to improvements in both the quality and availability of mobile homes in such retirement areas as California, Florida, and Arizona.

Characteristic of this phase is the attempt of widows to retain the housing they lived in before their partners died. Headship rates for widowed women aged 65-69 in 1960 were 28 percent lower than for married women of the same ages but were only 12 percent lower than the married group in 1980. The difference in homeownership rates for the same groups went from 42 percent to 28 percent. Like those who are divorced, widows can often keep their homes if they have sufficient equity in the house; other assets, as well as social security and SSI income, also help.

For those widows who maintained an independent household but did not remain homeowners, the most common adjustment was to move to apartments: 20 percent of the households headed by widows rented in 1980, compared with 11 percent of the married-couple households. Moreover, 22 percent of the widows in the late 1890s cohort did not head their own households. While many of this group lived with relatives (usually their children), a significant number also lived with non-relatives as either partners or boarders; some left households altogether to live in nursing homes or hospitals (and are excluded from the data presented here). According to the 1970 census, nine percent of 80-84-year-olds lived in nursing homes; the percentage for those below age 75, however, was much lower.

Implications for Forecasting

The cohort analysis described in this chapter provides an important tool for forecasting housing consumption for various household and family types over time. Although the overall patterns are similar, different cohorts achieved different levels of headship and ownership as they passed through the same stages of the life cycle. Each successive group made more progress in the housing market in terms of headship, ownership, and occupancy of larger units than did the previous cohorts. Thus, cohort analysis provides the information on the continually improved housing of each particular cohort without which predictions of housing consumption must fall short.

Forecasts using cohort analysis require judgments about the likely continuation of past trends, using our best analysis of market factors. For instance, for many households in the 1970s getting ahead meant larger houses. As a result, by 1980 we observe a significant number of large units being occupied by married couples with one or no children. Whatever the causes of this divergence between family and house sizes, this trend raises many important questions for housing in the 1980s. Unlike the 1970s, we anticipate that increases in house values in the 1980s will be modest. Similarly, we anticipate that the real interest rates charged for home mortgages will be high compared to previous decades. Thus it remains to be seen whether cohorts that are getting ahead in this decade--a period of lower inflation in house prices, reduced affluence, and more expensive housing finance--will exhibit housing consumption patterns similar to those of preceding cohorts.

We expect that the demand for large units will probably lessen, as ownership of large homes increases less rapidly among the baby-boom cohorts than it did for the cohorts just ahead of them. Nonetheless, the baby-boom cohorts will not make a major shift away from larger homes. Many of these baby-boom families already have two children; in addition, they are moving into their peak earning years, and will have accumulated sufficient equity in their current units to permit them to trade up to larger homes. Thus despite continued housing affordability problems, many baby-boom households will still occupy large single-family detached homes.

The situation facing the nation's young adult population is somewhat more bleak. Cohorts under the age of 25 in 1980 lagged slightly behind previous cohorts at that age in rates of headship. If the rental housing market continues to tighten, the resulting trend toward delayed household formation would represent a striking break from the patterns of the 1960s and early 1970s.

Despite the slowdown in forming households, home-ownership among the young adults is nevertheless on a par with past experience. In 1980, almost twice as many households under age 30 owned large houses as did the same age group in 1960, while only half as many owned medium-sized houses; the number living in mobile homes also doubled. Although ownership of condominiums or cooperatives rose over the 20-year period, these types represented less than two percent of all units owned by 25-29-year-olds in 1980.

While young homeowners did benefit to a certain extent from the increase in house values and equity in recent years, young renter households had no similar advantages. As the cost of owning a home increased faster than renter household income, the difficulty of making the transition from renter to owner status increased. Continued high real interest rates will also make it much harder for young adults to get started in the 1980s. This is not to suggest that homeownership rates will drop precipitously. Rather, more young renters will buy mobile homes, condominiums, or other forms of owner-occupied housing rather than moving directly from apartments to single-family detached homes, as was the common pattern among earlier generations.

These predictions show how the cohort approach, unlike other methods, builds forecasts on a detailed assessment of the current housing patterns of each cohort. It is thus able to take into account the different ways in which projected economic conditions, such as high real mortgage interest rates, affect the housing choices of specific household types at different ages. These estimates of housing consumption can then be combined with predictions about household income and housing costs to produce a forecast of housing consumption in the 1980s.

NOTES

1. Census of Population and Housing, 1960, Public Use Sample (1-in-100), machine-readable file (Washington, DC: U.S. Government Printing Office, no date); Census of Population and Housing, 1970: Public Use Sample (1-in-100), machine-readable file (Washington, DC: U.S. Government Printing Office, no date); Annual Housing Survey, 1975 (National) machine-readable file, (Washington, DC: U.S. Government Printing Office, 1978); and Annual Housing Survey, 1980, (National) machine-readable file (Washington, DC: U.S. Government Printing Office, 1982).

4

HOUSING STOCK ADJUSTMENTS

During the period from 1950 to 1980, the nation's housing inventory increased by more than 41 million units. Over the three decades, 52 million new units were built; these new additions were offset by the net losses of 11 million from the existing stock. These simple statistics, however, mask the complex process by which the housing inventory changes over time. While new construction and mobile home placements accounted for the largest share of growth, conversions of single-family structures into two or more units, and of nonresidential buildings into residential space, also added significant numbers to the total inventory. Housing losses are most often due to demolitions, fires, floods, and other natural disasters, but they also result from the merger of two units into one or the conversion of a residential unit to a nonresidential use.

Non-new construction additions to the inventory compete directly with conventional new construction activities. Conversion of single-family homes into multi-family structures, for example, reduces the need for new construction, as does the conversion of nonresidential structures into residential units. Since conversion adds primarily to the multi-family stock, continued growth in such non-new construction additions could have a substantial effect on this sector of the housing industry.

After discussing the historical relationship between new construction and changes in the total housing inventory, this chapter presents estimates of new construction and non-new construction additions as well as inventory losses in the 1970s for each of the four major census regions. The chapter also reviews the problems of using decennial census and Annual Housing Survey data to analyze the components of inventory change. Despite the limitations of available data, it is clear that a dramatic decline in inventory losses and rapid growth in non-new construction additions occurred over the last decade, changes that have important implications for future housing construction and investment activity.

Historical Trends in Inventory Adjustment

Converting simple census statistics into estimates of components of inventory change must be done with caution. The definitions of inventory losses and non-new construction additions change over time, as does the ability of the Census Bureau to measure these shifts. It is therefore useful to begin with a simple analysis of changing patterns of new construction and net losses.

Net losses are defined as total losses from all causes (fire, demolition, remodeling, etc.) minus non-new construction additions (conversion, rehabilitation, etc.), also referred to as "other" additions. Total inventory change is thus equal to new construction activity (conventional new construction plus mobile home placements) minus net losses. The decennial census provides relatively accurate information on total inventory change, and equally accurate measures of new construction activity are also readily available. Thus, the estimate of net losses is computed as a residual and does not depend on the ability of the Census Bureau to measure losses or non-new construction additions.

The data in Table 4.1 indicate that after increasing by 26.4 percent in the 1950s, the total inventory grew by only 16.7 percent in the 1960s, but by more than 26 percent in the 1970s. While the number of new construction additions in the 1960s rose slowly compared to the 1950s, new construction in the 1970s added more than 2 million units per year to the inventory. Net losses also varied considerably from one decade to the next. In the 1960s, the demolition of units for highway construction, urban renewal, and other public uses, combined with high levels of abandonment in inner cities, produced unprecedented net loss rates: more than 6.5 million units, or 10.9 percent of the housing stock at the beginning of the decade. In contrast, net

Table 4.1

COMPONENTS OF INVENTORY CHANGE, 1950-1980

Component	Number of Units (thousands)			Percentage of Beginning Stock		
	1950-60	1960-70	1970-80	1950-60	1960-70	1970-80
Beginning-of-decade Stock	47,538	60,134	70,184	100.0	100.0	100.0
Total Change	12,596	10,050	18,376	26.4	16.7	26.2
New Construction	16,034	16,616	20,938	33.7	27.6	29.8
Net Loss	3,438	6,566	2,562	7.2	10.9	3.7
End-of-decade Stock	60,134	70,184	88,560	126.4	116.7	126.2

NOTE: Undercounted total stock estimated at 3.0 percent in 1950, 3.1 percent in 1960, 2.2 percent in 1970, and assumed to be 0.75 percent in 1980. New construction includes completed units plus placements of mobile homes.

SOURCE: New construction for 1970-1980 from U.S. Bureau of the Census, Construction Reports, series C-22. New construction for 1950-1960 and 1960-1970 from U.S. Bureau of the Census, Components of Inventory Change, 1950-1959 and 1960-1970 (Washington, DC: U.S. Government Printing Office).

losses during the 1970s amounted to only about 2.5 million
units, at a rate of 3.7 percent.

The demise of the urban renewal and inner-city highway
construction programs is only one reason for the reduction
in housing losses in the past decade. In the 1970s, the
rising cost of new construction, the growing demand for
housing in selected inner-city neighborhoods, and the
changing mixture of federal housing assistance programs
all helped to encourage the retention and more intensive
use of the existing stock. As federal, state, and local
policy makers came to realize, it was more economical to
renovate housing units than to remove and replace them.
Rather than continuing to add more subsidized new construction to weak inner-city housing markets, federal programs
in the 1970s shifted toward rental assistance and housing
rehabilitation.[1]

Demographic factors also played an important role in
reducing net housing losses. Declining household size
spurred the division of better-quality single-family homes
into two or more units. Although conversions to multi-
family use had occurred in older inner cities in the 1950s
and 1960s, they had often involved the subdivision of
low-quality dwelling units in declining neighborhoods. In
the 1970s, conversion activity spread to the suburbs,
indeed to any place that had a stock of large single-family
dwelling units. Reuse of nonresidential structures also
increased, as developers converted abandoned schools, warehouses, and factories into fashionable condominiums and
luxury apartments. Unlike the conversion activity in
previous decades, however, many of the subdivisions in the
1970s produced units that could compete successfully with
newly constructed housing in meeting the growing demand of
small, high-income households.[2]

The estimates of inventory change presented in Table
4.1 require several qualifications. Although the decennial
census represents a relatively complete enumeration of the
nation's households and housing units, it nonetheless
failed to count some occupied and vacant units. Post-
enumeration analysis suggests that the 1970 census missed
900,000 occupied and 600,000 vacant units, or 2.2 percent
of the total inventory. As Table 4.2 indicates, the adjusted count for 1970 was thus 70.2 million housing
units.[3] While post-enumeration analyses were less
sophisticated for earlier censuses, the Census Bureau did
estimate undercount rates of 3.0 and 3.1 percent for 1950
and 1960, respectively. The best estimate for the 1980

population under count is one-third the rate of 1970. Assuming that the improvement in the coverage of units is proportional to the improvement in the coverage of people, this means that the undercount rate for housing units fell to 0.75 percent.[4]

Since differential undercounts can seriously distort the relative effects of individual components of change, the estimates presented in Table 4.1 incorporate the adjustments. According to published census statistics, for example, the nation's housing stock grew from 68.7 million units in 1970 to 87.9 million units in 1980, an increase of 19.2 million units. Almost 850,000 units of this increase, however, are due to the Census Bureau's success in reducing undercount, producing a 4.5 percent exaggeration of the actual growth in housing units. Estimates of net losses are even more sensitive to assumptions about differential undercount: Without adjustment, the amount of net loss presented in Table 4.1 would have been 850,000 units lower, a difference of nearly one-third.

Table 4.2

UNDERCOUNT OF TOTAL HOUSING INVENTORY, 1950-1980
(thousands of units)

Year	Adjusted Total	Enumerated by Census	Not Counted	Not Counted as Percentage Enumerated (%)
1950	47,538	46,137	1,401	3.00
1960	60,134	58,326	1,808	3.10
1970	70,184	68,672	1,512	2.20
1980	88,560	87,901	659	0.75

SOURCE: U.S. Bureau of the Census, 1970 Census of Population and Housing, The Coverage of Housing in the 1970 Census; and U.S. Bureau of the Census, The Post-Enumeration Survey: 1950 (Washington, DC: U.S. Government Printing Office). See also George Masnick and John Pitkin, The Changing Population of States and Regions (Cambridge, MA: The Joint Center for Urban Studies of MIT and Harvard University, 1982).

The accuracy of net loss figures for the decade also depends on the reliability of the measurement of new construction additions. Although the Census Bureau uses elaborate procedures to develop a sample of newly built units, coverage problems undoubtedly exist, especially in many low-density, non-metropolitan areas. Given the strategy used to locate and count new construction activity in a large sample of political jurisdictions, the Census Bureau's estimate of new construction activity probably differs from the actual count by less than 5.0 percent. Yet even if these many newly constructed units were missed, the number of net losses for the decade would be no higher than 3.8 million. Since the total inventory in 1970 was 70.2 million units, the upper-bound estimate of the net loss rate over the decade would therefore be only 5.5 percent, still well below the rates of 7.2 percent in the 1950s and 10.9 percent in the 1960s.

Review of Available Data

The census report of new construction understates both total inventory additions and total construction expenditures by including only units built on vacant land or new mobile home placements.[5] While such categories add the most units to the housing inventory, non-new construction additions can also increase the stock significantly. As Table 4.3 indicates, existing structures contributed to the creation of additional residential units. For example, a large single-family home may be converted into two or more apartments, or a waterfront warehouse into luxury condominiums. Conversions may entail complete rehabilitation that costs as much as or more than new construction, or they may involve only minor structural change such as adding a separate entrance or a new kitchen. In cases requiring large capital expenditures, it may be difficult to distinguish between a converted and a newly constructed unit.[6]

Another problem is the way the census defines the existing housing stock. Before 1980, decennial census counts did not include vacant mobile homes as part of the housing inventory. Thus, if a family moved into a vacant mobile home, pre-1980 census statistics recorded this move as a non-new addition to the stock rather than a reduction in the vacancy rate. Similarly, structures occupied by large groups of unrelated individuals (including dormitories, prisons, and hospitals, as well as single-family

Table 4.3

COMPONENTS OF ADDITIONS AND LOSSES TO THE INVENTORY

Additions to the Inventory

  New additions

    Conventional new construction on vacant land

    Placement of a new mobile home unit

  Other additions

    Conversion of one unit into two or more units

    Conversion of nonresidential into residential space

    Conversion of uninhabitable unit into inhabitable unit

    Occupancy of a vacant mobile home or movement of a
      previously occupied mobile home to a new site

    Occupancy of a group quarters unit by a family or single
      individual

Losses to the Inventory

  Demolition and disaster

  Merger

  Conversion to nonresidential use

  Condemnation to be demolished or as uninhabitable

  Vacancy of mobile home

  Occupancy of unit as group or transient quarters

  Removal of mobile home from site

SOURCE: U.S. Bureau of the Census, Annual Housing Survey,
Part A, General Housing Characteristics, 1980 (Washington, DC:
U.S. Government Printing Office).

houses rented by groups of unrelated individuals) are also
not considered part of the housing inventory. If a family
moves into a dwelling unit previously occupied by six or
more unrelated individuals, census statistics record the
transaction as a non-new construction addition.

Inventory losses result from a complex set of causes.
Some loss categories are clear: Units that are demolished
or are destroyed by fire, flood, or other natural disasters
are no longer available for occupancy. Other losses are of
a less permanent nature, for example, the conversion of
residential units into nonresidential use or the merger of
two or more units into a single home. Conversion or merger
activity that involves only limited capital expenditures
(such as opening up a stairway, unlocking an interior door,
or other minor changes), can easily be reversed.

Before publication of the Annual Housing Survey (AHS),
most analysts overlooked the transitory nature of some
units in the housing inventory. Because the survey returns
each year to the same sample of approximately 60,000 housing units, it is well suited to identify temporary losses.
The AHS data presented in Table 4.4 indicate that demolition and disaster losses account for only a small subset of
all units removed from the inventory during any given year:
more units were converted to nonresidential uses between
October 1976 and October 1977 than were demolished or lost
to fire, flood, or other natural disasters.

The AHS data also revealed problems with the census
treatment of mobile homes. As noted earlier, some mobile
home losses simply represent the change from occupancy to
vacancy rather than the actual destruction of a unit. In
other instances, a mobile home unit may be moved from one
site to another, which the Annual Housing Survey counts as
a loss in one location and a non-new construction addition
in another. With the recent growth in the number of mobile
home units, these accounting losses (i.e., losses that do
not involve destruction of a unit) have increased. As
Table 4.4 shows, during the year beginning October 1976,
mobile homes moved from one site to another account for
12.0 percent of all housing units counted as losses, and
31.9 percent of all previously owner-occupied housing
losses.

Over a short period of time, temporary losses from the
housing stock tend to be high relative to permanent losses;
over a full decade, however, temporary gains and losses
tend to cancel. For example, a unit could be counted as a
loss in the statistics for 1970-1973, then as an addition

Table 4.4

ESTIMATED HOUSING INVENTORY LOSSES BY PREVIOUS TENURE
OR STATUS AND TYPE OF LOSS, OCTOBER 1976-OCTOBER 1977
(thousands of units)

| Type of Loss | Total Losses | Previous Tenure or Status | | |
		Owner Occupied	Renter Occupied	Vacant
Retrievable Losses				
Temporary or Retrievable Losses	706	95	406	205
Converted to Nonresidential Use	300	54	154	92
Condemned to be Demolished	77	6	65	6
Exposed to Elements or Fire-damaged	329	35	187	107
Other Temporary Status				
Used as Group or Transient Quarters[a]	146	15	80	51
Total Retrievable	852	110	486	256
Permanent Losses				
Permanent Losses of Normal Types	430	163	209	58
Eliminated in Structural Conversion	17	3	10	4
Demolished	136	27	83	26
Destroyed by Disaster (fire, flood, tornado, etc.)	34	18	15	1
Lost through Merger	61	7	44	10
Other Permanent Loss	182	108	57	17
Other Change in Status[b]				
Unit Moved from Site	174	128	40	6
Total Permanent	604	291	249	64
Total Losses	1,456	401	735	320

a. Not defined as housing units, so counted here as an inventory
loss.

b. Defined as a loss at the vacated site, and an addition at the
new site.

SOURCE: Annual Housing Survey, 1977, national unpublished data,
compiled and analyzed by HUD, Housing and Demographic Analysis Division. See Duane McGough, "Housing Inventory Losses as a Requirement
for New Construction," a paper prepared for Economic Commission for
Europe, Seminar on Housing Forecasting and Programming, January 1981.

in the period 1973-1980. This factor could be significant
in areas with high numbers of mobile homes, group quarters,
marginally habitable seasonal units, or other types that
the census excludes from the inventory. Failing to recognize this difficulty, numerous analysts have combined loss
estimates for 1970-1973, the initial year of the AHS, with
those for 1973-1980. This procedure overstates both total
losses and the number of non-new construction additions for
the decade, leading to the incorrect conclusion that losses
in the 1970s are nearly as high as those estimated for the
1960s in the components of inventory change.[7]

Both the design of the AHS sample and the failure of
the Census Bureau to adjust for differential undercount
hamper the estimation of losses and non-new construction
additions.   The Annual Housing Survey tracks an initial
sample of units, augmenting the number each year to reflect
new construction, mobile home placements, and non-new construction additions.   While building permits provide a
relatively reliable source for conventional new construction, the Census Bureau was forced to employ a number of ad
hoc procedures to collect information on mobile home placements and non-new construction, including doorto-door
canvassing in selected geographical areas.   Predictably,
determining the loss of a sample unit was easier than
searching for potential non-new additions of units that had
previously been lost from the inventory. Thus, since the
AHS can more easily track temporary losses than temporary
additions, the survey tends to overstate the share of
temporary losses in inventory change.

Although the Census Bureau repeatedly warned of problems with the measurement of losses and non-new additions,
evaluating the accuracy of the AHS data was impossible
until release of the 1980 census. As the comparison in
Table 4.5 demonstrates, the AHS estimate of the total 1980
housing inventory is approximately 600,000 units less than
the census estimate, and the count of the year-round inventory is nearly one million units less. Moreover, relative
to the census, the AHS overstates the number of owner-
occupied single-family units, and understates both owner-
and renter-occupied, large multi-family structures.   The
difference in owner-occupied units in structures with five
or more units is most striking: the AHS estimate of
850,000 units is only 61.4 percent of the census count.
This large discrepancy could be explained if the AHS had
failed to account for the non-new construction that added
much to the nation's housing stock over the 1970s.[8]

Table 4.5

COMPARISON OF ANNUAL HOUSING SURVEY AND 1980 CENSUS COUNT OF HOUSING INVENTORY

(thousands of units)

Structure Type	Total			Own			Rent		
	AHS	Census	AHS as Percentage of Census	AHS	Census	AHS as Percentage of Census	AHS	Census	AHS as Percentage of Census
Seasonal	1,986	1,641	121.0	--	--	--	--	--	--
Year-round	85,305	86,259	98.9	51,964	51,795	100.3	27,358	28,595	95.7
1 Attached	54,353	53,943	100.8	43,941	43,322	101.4	7,266	7,508	96.8
1 Detached	3,416	3,531	96.7	1,934	1,784	108.4	1,208	1,467	82.3
2-4	10,799	9,758	110.7	2,249	2,254	99.8	7,472	6,652	112.3
5+	13,047	15,212	85.8	850	1,385	61.4	10,712	12,202	87.8
Mobile	3,690	3,815	96.7	2,990	3,049	98.1	700	766	91.4
TOTAL	87,291	87,901	99.3	51,964	51,795	100.3	27,358	28,595	95.7

NOTE: AHS is average of Annual Housing Survey published figures for October 1979 and October 1980, producing an estimate for April 1980. AHS and Census figures both exclude vacant mobile homes, estimated at 510,000 units. Census figures are unadjusted for undercount, estimated at 660,000 units.

SOURCE: Census of Population and Housing, 1980: Provisional Estimates of Social, Economic, and Housing Characteristics (Supplementary Report PHC 80-S1-1), 1982 (Washington, DC: U.S. Government Printing Office).

Preliminary Estimates of Losses and Non-new
   ## Construction Additions

Using published Annual Housing Survey statistics, it is possible to estimate losses and non-new construction additions to the inventory for the 1970s. While some double-counting may exist in the measure of total losses due to the problem of temporary losses, the measure of permanent losses in the AHS is more reliable and thus provides a lower-bound estimate of units lost over the decade. Total losses for the periods 1970-1973 and 1973-1980, with some allowance for the return of units to the inventory, serve as an upper-bound estimate.

Based on the AHS loss estimates, Table 4.6 shows changes in the housing stock over the 1970s. Net losses are obtained by comparing new construction and total inventory change; other additions are then derived by subtracting net losses from gross losses. Any error in measuring gross losses will therefore show up as an error of equal magnitude in the measurement of other (non-new construction) additions. This procedure implies that other additions for the decade 1970-1980 could be no less than 2.7 million and no more than 3.9 million units.

Although there is a great deal of uncertainty about losses and non-new construction additions, the estimates presented in Table 4.6 do establish several important facts. Even using the higher of the two estimates, the loss rate in the 1970s is substantially lower than it was in the 1960s. The figures also suggest that the widely used AHS estimate of 4.9 million other additions for the period 1970-1980 is at least 1.0 million units too high. This overestimate results from a failure to adjust for differential undercount and from double-counting temporary losses for the periods 1970-1973 and 1973-1980.

While it is clear that the AHS data overstate the number of non-new construction additions, such additions are nonetheless an increasingly important source of inventory growth. During the 1960s, conversions of single-family homes into two or more units added only 57,000 units to the stock each year; data from the 1980 Components of Inventory Change (CINCH) Report, in contrast, indicate that conversions in the 1970s accounted for 77,000 new units per year. The CINCH statistics also show that the restoration of previously uninhabitable residential dwelling units added 21,000 units per year; the reuse of schools, warehouses,

Table 4.6

TWO ESTIMATES OF LOSSES AND
NON-NEW CONSTRUCTION ADDITIONS, 1970-1980

Component	Low Estimate		Most Likely Estimate	
	Thousands of units	Percentage of 1970 Stock	Thousands of units	Percentage of 1970 Stock
Beginning-of-decade Stock	70,184	100.5	70,184	100.0
Total Change	18,376	26.2	18,376	26.2
New Construction	20,938	29.8	20,938	29.8
Net Loss	2,562	3.7	2,562	3.7
Gross Loss	5,265	7.5	6,500	9.3
Non-new Construction Additions	2,703	3.9	3,938	5.6

NOTE: Beginning-of-decade stock, decade change, and new construction figures are from Table 4.1. "Low estimate" equals
estimated number of permanent losses. Higher loss figures are
based on published AHS estimates for 1970-1973 plus 1973-1980.
Losses for the period 1970-1973 have been adjusted to reflect
return of retrievable losses to the inventory.

SOURCE: Census of Population and Housing, 1970 and 1980; and
Annual Housing Survey, 1973-80 (Washington, DC: U.S. Government
Printing Office).

and other nonresidential structures contributed another 81,000 units; and the conversions of group quarters and miscellaneous structures added 80,000 units.[9]

In interpreting the estimates in Table 4.6, it is important to keep in mind the census definition of losses and non-new construction additions. The Census Bureau considers the movement of a mobile home from one site to another as a loss at its place of origin and a non-new construction addition at its destination. Preliminary CINCH estimates for 1973-1980 suggest that more than 200,000 mobile homes each year move from one location to another, thus adding 200,000 units to the AHS estimates of both annual losses and non-new construction additions. Many analysts fail to make this distinction and discuss the AHS estimates as if non-new construction additions were synonymous with conversions of single-family homes and other activities that add units to the conventional inventory.

Because of the confusing treatment of mobile homes and other methodological problems, some analysts reject Census Bureau claims that other additions were an important source of growth in the 1970s. The 1980 CINCH statistics, however, place the number of non-new construction additions at 259,000 a year, a figure that corresponds closely to the lower-bound estimate for the decade of 2.7 million units shown in Table 4.6. Indeed, given the difficulty of identifying such additions, the CINCH estimate is likely to understate the actual number. Even these lower-bound estimates mean that non-new construction additions in the 1970s increased substantially from the estimated 1.3 million units recorded in the previous decade.

Regional Changes

Recent data suggest that household growth and housing construction have become increasingly scattered across a variety of locations. Along with the general shift from frostbelt to sunbelt and from central city to suburbs, the 1970s also witnessed the movement of population and jobs from larger metropolitan areas to smaller cities, towns, and rural areas. In the 1960s, 44 percent of the nation's more than 3,000 counties lost population, in both low-density rural areas and congested central cities. In the 1970s, only 18 percent of all counties lost population; among the 800 counties shifting from population loss to population gain were many low-density and largely rural areas, some experiencing growth for the first time in decades.

Employment redistribution has a major impact on migration patterns. In the 1970s, the growth of job opportunities in the sunbelt and in small cities and towns throughout the country coincided with movement of the retired population to these same areas. Advances in communications technology also enhanced the job growth potential of more remote locations. These forces combined to create a pattern of decentralized population growth, reversing decades of concentrated growth in a few of the largest metropolitan areas.

There is little reason to believe that any significant change in these trends will occur in the 1980s. The effect of such population shifts on the level of new construction and on the use of the existing housing stock, however, is not easy to predict. In even the slow-growth regions of the country, a decline in the average number of persons per household will continue to generate some demand for new housing construction.

Intra-regional population shifts will also stimulate additional housing construction in slow-growth areas. While expansion of the housing inventory in the Northeast and North Central regions continues to lag behind that of the rest of the country, pockets of strong housing construction activity do exist in these areas. As the data in Table 4.7 show, in the 1970s the housing inventory grew at a rate exceeding the national average in the non-metropolitan portion of the Northeast, the suburbs of small SMSAs of the Northeast region (Standard Metropolitan Statistical Areas) and all suburbs of the North Central regions.

In contrast to the Northeast and North Central regions, the large metropolitan areas of the South and West grew dramatically in the 1970s and will continue to expand in the 1980s. Even in these regions, however, the most rapid growth tends to be in the non-metropolitan areas and the smaller SMSAs. Because the non-metropolitan areas are so widely scattered, it is easy to underestimate the size of these markets. Throughout the 1970s, the media focused attention on certain fast-growth metropolitan areas, including Atlanta, Dallas, Houston, Miami, Tampa, San Diego, and Anaheim; collectively, the housing inventory in these seven cities increased by 2.2 million units over the decade. During the same period, the housing inventory increased in the non-metropolitan South by 2.5 million units, and by 1.1 million units in the non-metropolitan West.

Table 4.7

CHANGE IN TOTAL HOUSING INVENTORY BY
REGION AND TYPE OF LOCATION, 1970-1980

Type of Location	North-East	North-Central	South	West	Total
Central Cities					
Large SMSAs	0.3	-1.6	20.0	16.3	6.7
Medium SMSAs	2.5	8.2	28.0	42.2	20.8
Small SMSAs	12.6	19.6	28.3	61.7	27.8
Suburbs					
Large SMSAs	15.9	31.5	62.7	40.0	34.6
Medium SMSAs	25.5	34.4	55.6	76.2	44.3
Small SMSAs	30.2	31.8	58.0	54.5	45.3
Non-metropolitan Areas	28.8	22.8	35.0	55.2	32.4
TOTAL	14.7	20.3	39.9	42.0	28.7

NOTE: The 34 large SMSAs each had 1970 populations of
1.0 million or more. The 102 medium SMSAs had 1970 populations of from 250,000 to 1.0 million, while the 1,982 small
SMSAs had 1970 populations of less than 250,000. Numbers
in the table are unadjusted for the effect of differential
undercount on total housing inventory growth. Figures
exclude vacant mobile homes in 1970 but include them in
1980 totals.

SOURCE: Census of Population: Standard Metropolitan
Statistical Areas and Standard Consolidated Areas (supple-
mentary report PC 80-S1-5), 1980 (Washington, DC: U.S.
Government Printing Office).

Estimated Losses by Structure Type. Both the reduction of losses and the increase in non-new construction additions are market responses to the rising costs of housing capital and changes in demand as households become smaller. Because the characteristics of the existing stock vary across housing markets, how these national trends manifest themselves will also vary within and across regions. Forecasts of housing market activity in general, and of the components of inventory change in particular, must therefore rely on analyses that are disaggregated by structure type and location.

Based on AHS data for the period 1973-1980 and the Census Bureau's data on components of inventory change for the 1960s, Table 4.8 reveals that losses in both the single- and multi-family stock declined. In the 1960s, 21.3 percent of the beginning stock of two- to four-family structures was lost; in the 1970s, however, this rate dropped sharply to 13.3 percent. Equally pronounced was the decline in the loss rate for structures with five or more units. Even the relatively low loss rate for single-family units decreased.

The distributions in Table 4.8 also demonstrate the importance of disaggregated analysis. As the number of mobile homes rose over the 1970s, so too did the rate of mobile home losses and the significance of this rate to the total loss rate. These units accounted for 19.3 percent of all losses to the year-round inventory for the decade, up from 6.3 percent in the 1960s. Consequently, the loss rate for all year-round units in the 1970s was 9.1 percent, a figure that is significantly higher than the 7.6 percent estimated for the conventional inventory alone.

There are several other reasons for being especially careful about including data on mobile homes in estimates of inventory losses. As noted previously, while many mobile home units may have shorter useful lives than conventional units, mobile home losses are nonetheless exaggerated because the loss figures include both vacancies and movement from one site to another. Moreover, the share of mobile home units in the inventory not only varies over time, but also over regions. As Table 4.9 indicates, mobile home units accounted for 26.5 percent of housing losses in the South during the 1970s, but only 4.8 percent in the 1960s. Mobile homes contributed one-third of all losses in the rural South over the past decade, more than ten times the share of losses in central cities nationwide.

Table 4.8

DECADE LOSS RATES AND DISTRIBUTION
BY STRUCTURE TYPE, 1960-1980

Structure Type	Decade Loss Rate As Percentage of Total Inventory		Distribution of Losses (%)	
	1960-70	1970-80	1960-70	1970-80
Conventional	10.7	7.6	93.7	80.3
1 Unit	7.7	6.0	50.1	45.1
2-4 Units	21.3	13.3	27.0	18.7
5+ Units	17.0	10.5	16.6	17.0
Mobile Homes	55.6	42.0	6.3	19.3
TOTAL	11.3	9.1	100.0	100.0

NOTE: Conventional inventory is total year-round inventory less mobile homes. Estimates for 1970s derived from AHS data for that period. Thus $(1 + LD) = (1 + L73)^P$ where LD is the decade loss rate, L73 is the loss rate for seven-year period beginning October 1973, and p is an exponent equal to 10/7.

SOURCE: U.S. Bureau of Census, Annual Housing Survey, 1973 and 1980 (Washington, DC: U.S. Government Printing Office).

Since many of the errors in the measurement of housing losses involve mobile homes or seasonal and only marginally habitable units, loss estimates for the conventional year-round inventory are likely to be more accurate than those for the total inventory.[10] As Table 4.10 shows, losses from the conventional inventory of the central cities in the Northeast and North Central regions remained high in the 1970s, evidence of the continuing decline of these areas. This contrasts sharply, however, with the experience in the West and the South: in these regions, losses decreased in central-city areas as well as in suburban areas.

Table 4.9

LOSS RATE OF MOBILE HOME UNITS, 1960-1980
(as percentage of total year-round losses)

Region	Central City		Suburban		Non-SMSA		Total	
	1960-70	1970-80	1960-70	1970-80	1960-70	1970-80	1960-70	1970-80
Northeast	1.9	0.5	5.8	6.2	8.6	28.3	4.0	8.4
North Central	2.2	1.3	11.0	18.4	9.0	25.6	6.2	15.3
South	2.9	4.3	9.7	28.8	4.4	33.5	4.8	26.5
West	7.0	4.3	16.4	30.6	14.1	29.8	12.0	21.7
TOTAL	3.2	2.3	11.0	22.2	7.3	30.5	6.3	19.3

NOTE: Estimates for the 1970s derived from AHS data for period 1973-1980.

SOURCE: U.S. Bureau of the Census, Annual Housing Survey, 1973-1980 (Washington, DC: U.S. Government Printing Office).

Table 4.10

DECADE GROSS LOSS RATE FOR CONVENTIONAL INVENTORY, 1960-1980
(as percentage of initial stock)

Region	Central City		Suburban		Non-SMSA		Total	
	1960-70	1970-80	1960-70	1970-80	1960-70	1970-80	1960-70	1970-80
Northeast	10.6	11.9	5.4	3.6	6.7	6.6	7.8	7.3
North Central	13.0	10.9	7.0	4.0	9.8	9.1	10.2	7.9
South	15.6	8.1	10.2	6.1	13.1	11.5	13.3	9.0
West	12.3	6.1	8.9	3.2	15.2	9.8	11.5	5.5
TOTAL	12.9	9.4	7.5	4.2	11.3	9.4	10.7	7.6

NOTE: Conventional inventory is total year-round units less mobile homes. Estimates for the 1970s derived from AHS data for period 1973-1980.

SOURCE: U.S. Bureau of the Census, Components of Inventory Change, 1960 to 1970; U.S. Bureau of Census, Annual Housing Survey, 1973-1980 (Washington, DC: U.S. Government Printing Office).

The estimates in Table 4.10 thus demonstrate how broad national trends play themselves out in regional and metropolitan housing markets. Factors peculiar to these markets, such as the age and quality of the stock, modify the way in which national forces operate in a particular subregion. While 30 years of growth have left the United States with a relatively high-quality inventory, housing starts have not been evenly distributed across the country. As Table 4.11 shows, new housing tends to be concentrated in the faster-growing regions of the South and West. For the nation as a whole, 59.8 percent of all dwelling units existing in 1980 had been built since 1950. This proportion varies, however, from less than 28 percent in the central-city areas of the Northeast to nearly 79 percent in the suburban South and West.

Table 4.12 illustrates the high correlation between the age of a housing unit and the probability that the unit will be lost from the inventory. In the 1970s, losses of the pre-1950 stock amounted to 12.5 percent, compared to only 3.0 percent of post-1950 units. The difference in loss rates for old and new structures holds for each of the regions identified in the table.

Table 4.11

UNITS BUILT SINCE 1950 BY REGION
(as percentage of total year-round units in 1980)

Region	City	Suburb	Non-SMSA	Total
Northeast	27.9	51.9	44.9	42.2
North Central	38.0	69.7	46.5	53.7
South	63.2	81.9	66.5	70.2
West	61.2	79.0	66.4	70.5
TOTAL	47.9	70.7	57.8	59.8

SOURCE: U.S. Bureau of Census, Annual Housing Survey, 1980 (Washington, DC: U.S. Government Printing Office).

Table 4.12

DECADE LOSS RATE BY AGE OF STRUCTURE
(as percentage of initial stock)

Region	Central City		Suburbs		Non-SMSA		Total	
	Built Before 1950	Built After 1950	Built Before 1950	Built After 1950	Built Before 1950	Built After 1950	Built Before 1950	Built After 1950
Northeast	15.2	1.6	6.1	0.9	8.9	2.4	10.6	1.4
North Central	14.3	4.4	7.2	2.2	11.2	4.0	11.6	3.2
South	14.9	3.1	16.0	2.7	17.4	6.1	16.3	4.1
West	11.9	1.7	8.7	1.1	13.3	6.5	11.2	2.2
TOTAL	14.3	2.8	8.5	1.8	13.4	5.2	12.5	3.0

SOURCE: U.S. Bureau of the Census, Annual Housing Survey, 1973 and 1980 (Washington, DC: U.S. Government Printing Office).

The results presented in these tables are consistent with the findings of a recent study by the Congressional Budget Office (CBO).[11] The CBO analysis used AHS data to measure the quality of the housing inventory according to major problems in the plumbing and heating systems that are likely to require replacement, and less serious problems that can be repaired in the course of normal maintenance. As expected, the CBO study found a high incidence of inadequate housing in the larger central cities of the Northeast and North Central regions, as well as in certain rural areas, particularly in the South.

Simple economic theory suggests that the level of maintenance expenditures for a given unit depends on the cost of maintenance relative to the expected return. In depressed inner-city areas experiencing high vacancy rates and little growth in real rents, there may be little incentive to maintain property. As the unit deteriorates, the probability increases that it will be lost to the inventory. Even in a relatively fast-growing area, low-quality units will have a higher probability of loss.

Estimates of Other Additions by Structure Type.   By comparing AHS estimates of change in total inventory, new construction activity, and losses for the period from 1973 to 1980, it is possible to develop rough estimates of non-new construction additions by type and location. Since this procedure computes such additions as a residual, the estimates are highly sensitive to problems associated with differential undercount and the temporary shifting of units in and out of the inventory. As noted earlier, the 1970 census failed to enumerate 600,000 vacant units, many of which were seasonal homes; the 1973 AHS located even fewer seasonal vacancies, but subsequent improvement in coverage raised the number substantially. As a result of the higher number of seasonal vacancies, comparing the uncorrected census with the AHS data greatly overstates the number of non-new construction additions.

As Table 4.13 shows, the AHS data imply that non-new construction additions of seasonally vacant units were 2.5 times the number of the initial stock in 1970. Moreover, these figures state that seasonal vacancies accounted for 24.8 percent of all non-new construction additions for the decade. With mobile homes representing 11.1 percent, less than two-thirds of all non-new construction additions in the 1970s were thus part of the conventional housing inventory.

Table 4.13

NON-NEW CONSTRUCTION ADDITIONS BY STRUCTURE TYPE, 1970-1980

Structure Type	Percentage of Initial Stock	Distribution by Type (%)
Seasonal	258.7	24.8
Total Year-round	7.0	75.2
Mobile Home	23.8	11.1
Conventional	6.3	64.1
Single-Family	3.9	28.3
2-4 Units	16.5	22.6
5+ Units	8.4	13.2
TOTAL	9.3	100.0

NOTE: Decade   rate   estimated   using   data   for   period
1973-1980.   See Table 4.8 for explanation of methodology.

SOURCE: U.S. Bureau of Census, Annual Housing Survey,
1973-1980 (Washington, D.C: U.S. Government Printing
Office).

Table 4.14 shows, however, that non-new construction additions may have increased the conventional inventory by as much 6.3 percent in the 1970s. The rate of such additions is surprisingly uniform across the country, albeit somewhat higher in the faster-growing regions of the West and South. This is consistent with the observation that increases in these additions reflect in part the adjustment of the housing inventory to growth pressures. Even in slow-growth regions, though, the trend toward smaller households provides an incentive for investors to convert large single-family homes as well as nonresidential structures into smaller apartments and condominium units. Similiarly, the availability of attractive factory buildings and warehouses has promoted the conversion of such structures into residential space.

Table 4.14

ADDITIONS TO CONVENTIONAL INVENTORY BY REGION, 1970-1980
(as percentage of initial stock)

Region	Central City Total Additions	Central City Non-new Construction	Suburban Total Additions	Suburban Non-new Construction	Non-SMSA Total Additions	Non-SMSA Non-new Construction	Total Total Additions	Total Non-new Construction
Northeast	10.8	5.3	18.3	5.7	20.3	5.0	15.9	5.4
North Central	12.1	4.1	33.4	7.3	26.0	5.9	24.1	5.8
South	24.4	5.8	49.3	4.9	40.8	9.2	38.2	6.9
West	25.3	6.5	46.7	7.1	43.8	9.1	38.2	7.3
TOTAL	17.8	5.3	35.8	6.2	33.4	7.5	29.0	6.3

NOTE: Conventional inventory is total year-round inventory less mobile homes. Estimates for 1970s derived from AHS data for period 1973-1980.

SOURCE: U.S. Bureau of the Census, Annual Housing Survey, 1973-1980 (Washington, DC: U.S. Government Printing Office).

With the increase in other additions and the more intensive utilization of the existing inventory, new construction statistics have become poor measures of economic activity in the housing sector. In 1978 when housing starts were at a peak, the value of new residential construction put in place was $75.8 billion; an additional $37.5 billion was spent on residential alterations and repairs to the existing stock. Since that time, the value of new residential construction fell to $62.0 billion in 1982, while expenditures for alterations and repairs increased to $46.4 billion.[12]

Implications for Forecasting

While the growth of households described in Chapters 2 and 3 creates some demand for new housing, the amount of new construction required is also directly affected by the extent of housing preservation and adaptive reuse. Over the past decade, losses to the housing inventory have declined sharply, and non-new construction has become an increasingly important source supplying new housing. Non-new construction will continue to supplant a significant amount of new construction during the 1980s. For that reason, forecasters must explicitly model the removal, preservation, and reuse of the existing stock if they are to accurately predict new housing activity.

Finally, the national patterns of housing stock use must be examined on a regional basis. The non-metropolitan areas of the South do not have a large inventory of structures suitable for rehabilitation and renovation. Therefore, non-new construction will be less significant there than in other parts of the country. Similarly, high loss rates have continued in the large northern central cities in contrast to the declining national loss rate, reflecting the older stock and shrinking demand in northern central cities. In short, forecasters must recognize not only broad national trends but also regional variations in the preservation and reuse of the existing housing inventory.

NOTES

1. For an assessment of the effect of changing federal policy on metropolitan housing markets, see Anthony Downs, Neighborhoods and Urban Development (Washington, DC: The Brookings Institution, 1981).

2. For further discussion, see Phillip Clay, "Accessory Apartments" (paper prepared for the Lincoln Institute of Land Policy, Cambridge, MA, 1982).

3. U.S. Bureau of the Census, 1970 Census of Population and Housing, Estimates of Coverage of the Population by Sex, Age, and Race (Washington, DC: U.S. Government Printing Office, 1973).

4. George Masnick and John Pitkin, The Changing Population of States and Regions (Cambridge, MA: Joint Center for Urban Studies of MIT and Harvard University, 1982).

5. For a complete definition of each of the components of inventory change, see the introduction to U.S. Bureau of the Census, 1980 Annual Housing Survey, Part A, General Housing Characteristics (Washington, DC: U.S. Government Printing Office, 1982).

6. For a discussion of non-new construction statistics, see Duane McGough, Additions to the Housing Supply by Means Other than New Construction (Washington, DC: U.S. Department of Housing and Urban Development, 1982).

7. This procedure results in part from the way the Census Bureau presents summary statistics on inventory change in the Annual Housing Survey Reports. See, for example, Table B in the Introduction to the 1980 Annual Housing Survey.

8. At present, the Bureau of the Census is attempting to reconcile 1980 AHS and census data as a first step in analyzing components of inventory change for the past decade. Although there were plans to link 1970 and 1980 decennial census data to produce an analysis for the entire decade, budget cutbacks forced the bureau to abandon this effort. Instead, the components-of-change analysis will be based on AHS data and cover only the period 1973-1980. For

further assessment of problems associated with the use of decennial census data, see William C. Apgar, Jr., "The Use of 1980 Census Data for National Policy Research" (paper prepared for the U.S. Department of Housing and Urban Development, 1981).

9. U.S. Bureau of the Census, Census of Housing, Components of Inventory Change Survey, supplementary reports PC80-S1-2 (Washington, DC: U.S. Government Printing Office, 1983).

10. Analyses of new construction requirements rarely distinguish losses by type. In his otherwise excellent paper, for example, McGough discusses only total losses.

11. Congressional Budget Office, Federal Housing Policy: Current Programs and Recurring Issues (Washington, DC: U.S. Government Printing Office, 1978).

12. U.S. Bureau of the Census, Survey of Residential Alterations and Repairs, construction report C-50; and The Value of New Construction Put in Place, construction report C-30, various years (Washington, DC: U.S. Government Printing Office.

5

HOUSING MARKET DYNAMICS IN THE 1970s

This chapter integrates the preceding analyses by examining the results of the market operation in response to changes in patterns of housing demand. The discussion begins with a description of national trends in homeownership and housing characteristics. The following sections focus on changes in housing prices and rents and issues of affordability. The final section considers regional variations in housing markets due to different growth rates over the decade.

Changing Uses of the Housing Stock

During the 1970s, 18.4 million units were added to the nation's housing stock, an increase of 26 percent. While it was not the century's largest gain in units, it is nonetheless a major increment. In some regions of the country, particularly the rural areas, this growth represents a significant reversal of trends.

An important indication of change in the use of the housing stock is the homeownership rate. In 1940, 44 percent of households owned their homes; by 1970, however, 62.8 percent of households were homeowners. As Table 5.1 indicates, a modest gain of 1.6 percentage points in the homeownership rate also occurred during the 1970s. This increase is noteworthy given the demographic changes of the decade: the extraordinary growth in the number of small,

Table 5.1

SELECTED NATIONAL HOUSING CHARACTERISTICS, 1970-1980

Characteristics	1970	1980	Change (%)
Total Units (millions)	70.2	88.4	26
Ownership Rate (percentage of households)	62.8	64.4	3
Type of Occupied Units at Address (percentage of total units)			
1 Unit	69.7	71.3	2
2-9 Units	17.8	14.0	-21
10+ Units	10.4	10.1	- 3
Mobile Homes	2.4	4.6	92
Median Value of Owner Units	$19,500	$55,800	186
Median Rents	$101	$210	108

SOURCE: Census of Population and Housing (Washington, DC: U.S. Government Printing Office, 1970 and 1980).

young, and nonfamily households would suggest instead a reduction in overall ownership.

Over the decade, the press drew a great deal of attention to the gentrification and rehabilitation of the central-city housing stock. The evidence on the aggregate changes in structure types, however, indicates that the trend toward higher-density, urban living was overstated at best. First, single-family units, rather than declining in share, showed a slight increase from 70 to 71 percent of all housing.   Second, large multi-family structures declined from 10.4 percent of the 1970 housing stock to 10.1 percent of the 1980 stock; structures with two to nine units represented less than one percent of the new units added during the 1970s. Third, mobile homes contributed 13 percent of the units added to the nation's housing stock, accounting for 4.6 percent of the total inventory in 1980.

Changes to the housing stock witnessed over the decade were the result of continuing decentralization of new construction activity. While some high-density development did occur in large cities, most housing stock growth was in single-family structures, at low density and located in smaller metropolitan and non-metropolitan areas.

The median value for all owner-occupied units increased substantially from $19,500 in 1970 to $55,800 in 1980, considerably more than the 131 percent increase in the general consumer price index. Part of the increase in median value reflects an improvement in the quality of the housing stock, and part reflects the real inflation in housing prices. The rapid inflation in housing prices caused genuine concern about long-term problems of housing affordability. There was also a great deal of public discussion and concern about rising rents and the affordability of rental housing. These issues were raised in spite of the fact that median rents increased by less than the general consumer price index. These questions of affordability are discussed in more detail in the following section.

The Costs of Housing

Homeownership

The decision to buy a home or condominium unit involves a substantial and complex financial commitment.[1] While the actual purchase price of the unit is of course central, the cash cost of homeownership also entails several ongoing expenses, including mortgage interest payments, fuel and utility costs, maintenance and repairs, real estate taxes, and insurance. In addition to out-of-pocket outlays, the loss of income as interest yield from the homeowner's down payment or accumulated equity indirectly raises costs. The deductibility of interest and property taxes from taxable income, however, directly reduces costs while the expectation of appreciation allows an indirect reduction. Changes in cash, direct, or indirect costs can thus affect the total cost of homeownership facing potential buyers.

Throughout the decade there was great controversy about trends in the cost of homeownership. Figure 5.1 illustrates how homeownership costs have changed relative to income. Between 1965 and 1973, both cash and direct housing costs roughly kept pace with median income. Between

Figure 5.1

HOMEOWNERHSIP COSTS AS PERCENTAGE
OF MEDIAN FAMILY INCOME, 1965–1983

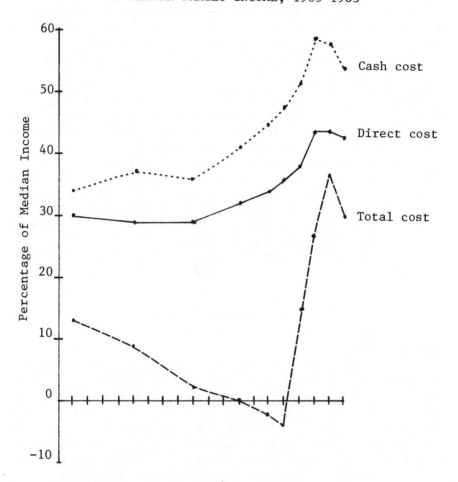

Cash cost: out-of-pocket costs, including
mortgage, utilities, maintenance, taxes, and insurance; Direct cost: cash cost net of tax saving;
Total cost: total cash cost net of tax saving and
expected capital gain, including forgone interest
on equity.

SOURCE: H. James Brown et al., "Homeownership
and Housing Affordability in the United States, 1963–
1983" (Cambridge, MA: Joint Center for Urban Studies
of MIT and Harvard University, 1983).

1973 and 1979, the cash costs of homeownership began to increase but at a relatively modest pace; total costs, in
contrast, fell relative to income as homebuyers justifiably
anticipated capital gains once they "got into the market."
While there is little evidence from total costs of an
affordability crisis in the early part of the decade, cash
costs had climbed to nearly 50 percent of median income by
1979 while total costs rose from zero to 36 percent of
income.

The change in total homeownership costs can best be
understood by examining particular cost components for
several time periods. As Table 5.2 shows, home prices rose
significantly faster than prices in general between 1963
and 1973; mortgage interest rates remained between 6.0 and
8.0 percent, while fuel and utility costs rose only
moderately. The cash cost of homeownership remained at
about one-third of median family income. From 1963 to
1973, existing homes appreciated in value at an average
annual rate of 7.5 percent; housing production rose significantly, peaking in 1972 at over 2.3 million starts or
more than 30 percent higher than the new construction level
in 1964.

In 1973 and 1974, the U.S. economy experienced rapid
inflation for the first time in modern history. When the
Federal Reserve Board responded with a tight monetary
policy, the country slid into a deep recession that hit
bottom in May 1975 with over 9.0 percent of the labor force
unemployed. Although new construction activity decreased
dramatically, the housing market remained remarkably
stable: consumer prices, home values, maintenance costs,
and homeownership costs all rose at about the same rate.
Due to higher mortgage rates and substantial increases in
utility costs, however, the total direct costs of homeownership rose from about 29 to 32 percent of income.

During the construction boom between 1975 and 1979,
housing prices rose at a rate of 12.3 percent annually
while consumer prices increased only 7.5 percent. Mortgage
rates edged up by less than two points in four years, and
the cash costs of homeownership relative to income grew
only modestly. Anticipated capital gains actually made
total homeownership costs negative.

To combat inflation and the growth of the money supply,
the Federal Reserve Board again took strong measures in
November 1979. The prime rates rose from 11.0 to over 20.0
percent; in just two years, conventional mortgage rates

Table 5.2

CHANGES IN HOUSING PRICES AND COSTS, 1963-1982
(as percentage changes)

Prices and Costs	1963-73	1973-75	1975-79	1979-82
Average Annual Changes				
All Consumer Prices[a]	3.8	10.0	7.5	10.2
Cash Cost of Homeownership[b]	5.1	11.0	9.5	13.7
New Home Prices	6.2	11.1	12.3	2.2
Existing Home Prices	7.5	10.6	12.3	6.5
Fuel & Utility Prices	2.5	15.0	9.1	13.4
Maintenance & Repair Costs	NA	11.5	8.0	9.1
Average Mortgage Interest Rate[c]				
Low	5.9	7.8	8.9	10.7
High	7.8	9.6	10.9	16.4

a. Annual rate of change in the Consumer Price Index.
b. Annual change in broad-based index of cash costs to homeowners including purchase price, mortgage interest, fuel and utilities, insurance, maintenance and repair costs, etc.
c. Actual average conventional mortgage rates on single-family homes sold. Figures are highest and lowest monthly average for periods given beginning and ending in July (Lexington, MA: Data Resources, Inc., U.S. Central Data Banks).

SOURCES: U.S. Bureau of the Census, New One-Family Homes Sold and For Sale (Current Construction Reports, series C-25) (Washington, DC: U.S. Government Printing Office, 1963-1983). National Association of Realtors, "Median Sales Price Existing Homes for the U.S." (1968-73 only). U.S. Department of Labor, Bureau of Labor Statistics, Consumer Price Index: Fuel and Utilities and Maintenance and Repair (Washington, DC: U.S. Government Printing Office).

rose by approximately six points. Following the oil short-age in 1979, fuel and utility costs also increased rapidly. Homeownership costs grew nearly 50 percent, or 30 percent faster than consumer prices and incomes.

While many commentators have offered simple explana-tions for the affordability crisis, the current situation has its roots in a number of complex and interrelated changes that have occurred in the last decade. Among the major factors that have contributed to the crisis are changes in the mortgage market, higher interest rates, inflation, demographic trends, and government regulation.

The most important causes of high mortgage rates have been the rising federal deficits and the resulting monetary policies of the Federal Reserve Board. After the Federal Reserve Board moved to reduce the amount of credit in the system in November 1979, short-term interest rates rose rapidly, with long-term rates following close behind.

Table 5.3

INVESTMENT AND GROSS NATIONAL PRODUCT, 1960–1983

Period	Total Investment as Percentage of GNP	Residential Investment as Percentage of Total Investment	Residential Investment as Percentage of GNP
1960–65	14.3	33.3	4.8
1965–70	14.6	27.0	3.9
1970–75	14.8	29.7	4.4
1975	13.7	25.9	3.6
1975–80	15.3	29.0	4.5

NOTE: Total investment is gross private domestic in-vestment.

SOURCE: Department of Commerce, Bureau of Economic Analysis (Washington, DC: U.S. Government Printing Office).

The statistics in Table 5.3 suggest that the relative ability of housing to compete for funds in national capital markets has also changed. Except during the two major recessions in 1975 and 1982, private domestic investment has remained as a remarkably constant share of the gross national product; indeed, its portion actually rose between 1975 and 1980. Housing's share of investment, however, fell from 33 to 29 percent. The innovations in financial markets have heightened the competition for capital between residential and non-residential uses. While greater competition should result in a more efficient use of available resources, the housing market has clearly suffered from changes in the thrift industry.[2]

During the period 1974-1979, the most significant cause of higher ownership costs was rapid inflation in home prices due primarily to the rising expectations of housing demanders. For 20 years, house values have run ahead of consumer prices and offered an important tax-sheltered investment opportunity. Since consumers tend to perceive housing as both an investment and a consumption good, their willingness to pay reflects both the worth of the housing purchased and the value of the expected capital gain.[3]

Demographic trends have also contributed indirectly to higher housing prices. As detailed in Chapter 2, in the 1970s the number of young adults aged 20-34 increased over 40 percent. Since many of these young adults have chosen to live independently, the total number of households, and therefore housing demand, has grown substantially.

Another source of higher housing prices has been the rising cost of complying with land use restrictions, building codes, and environmental regulations. While some analysts have argued that as much as 20 percent of new home costs may be attributable to compliance with such regulations, others assert that government restrictions actually drive down land values and have had only a very small effect on housing prices.[4]

Those who made the transition to homeownership in the mid-1970s bought into a booming market and managed to earn large, essentially tax-free capital gains. Those who failed to make the transition and new households entering the market for the first time, in contrast, have faced increasingly unfavorable conditions. Younger and poorer households are now less likely to own their own homes than they were five years ago. Those that have been able to purchase houses are much more likely to have selected condominiums or mobile homes than they were previously.

Those that were able to afford the traditional single-family detached home are seemingly more likely to have selected a smaller unit with fewer amenities.

Renting

The President's Commission and numerous other studies have noted that the costs of renting have not increased as rapidly as the costs of other consumer goods.[5] Table 5.4 illustrates the type of comparisons that have been done to make this point. The first column gives the percentage change in the consumer price index (CPI) for all items (excluding shelter costs), and the second the change in the consumer index for residential rents. From 1970 to 1980, the CPI for all items (excluding shelter) increased by 106.6 percent while the residential rent index increased by only 73.3 percent.

Unfortunately, the CPI residential rent index is not an accurate measure of changes in real rents because it does not account for depreciation of the housing and does not include all of the costs of renting, such as fuel or utility expenses. Column 3 of Table 5.4 presents a measure developed by Ira Lowry to index the total or gross cost of renting by including fuel and utility costs.[6] Lowry's index for 1970 to 1980 shows a much larger increase in the cost of renting (102.7 percent) as compared to the CPI rent index (73.3 percent). Still, even according to this more comprehensive measure of rental costs, real rents declined in the decade. As a result, renting has become an increasingly attractive alternative, and renters were paying less on average by the end of the decade.

At the same time, there has been substantial public concern and public policy debate over the "rental crisis." Cases have been documented of individual households that were unable to pay the required rents out of their limited income. Further, many cities and states have passed rent control legislation, severe restrictions on evictions, and controls or outright bans on condominium conversions in an effort to stop rising rents. The apparent contradiction of falling national real rents and growing public concern about the "rental crisis" makes clear two important qualifications to conclusions about national median rent.

First, while the average renter may be better off because the average rent fell in relation to other prices and renter median income, it does not follow that all renting households have improved their situation. Part of

Table 5.4

CHANGES IN PRICE INDEXES, 1960-1980
(as percentage changes)

Period	Consumer Price Index[a]	CPI Residential Rent[b]	Adjusted Rent Index[c]
1960-70	28.7	20.1	25.7
1960-65	6.4	5.6	7.8
1965-70	20.9	13.6	16.5
1970-80[d]	106.6	73.3	102.7
1970-75	39.1	24.7	34.3
1975-80[d]	48.5	40.0	50.9
1960-80[d]	165.8%	108.1%	154.7%

NOTE: All figures are percentage changes.

a. All items less shelter.
b. CPI for residential rent.
c. CPI residential rent index adjusted for depreci-
    ation (Lowry Index).
d. Data for 1980 are for the month of June; all other
    data are annual averages.

SOURCE: Ira S. Lowry, "Inflation Indexes for Rental
Housing," (Santa Monica, CA: Rand Corporation, 1982), Table
A.10, p. 30.

the concern about the "rental crisis" reflects a concern
for those households whose income does not permit them to
maintain adequate housing. Concern for these individuals
is the basis for rental assistance programs presently
implemented in many states and at the federal level.

Second, although the national average rent rose more
slowly than the average consumer price index, there was a
great deal of variation in local housing markets across the
nation. As described later in this chapter, analysis of
rent changes in counties with different household growth

rates indicates that fast-growing counties in fact experienced rent increases above the rate of general price inflation, while those undergoing little development showed slower increases. The average national rent change is useful information but does not tell the story for all households or all markets.

A further difficulty results from comparing changes in median income and median rent. This comparison implicitly assumes that the group of renters remains the same over time. Actually, the group of renters changes substantially, as higher-income renters are the most likely to become homeowners. This shift affects both the median income and the ratio of median rent to median income of renters. Further, rising income and falling real rents have enabled an increasing number of both young singles and older individuals to establish independent living arrangements. Single-person households (especially women) typically spend a higher proportion of their income on housing. Thus the increase in the number of single-person households increases the median rent-to-income ratio for the entire renting population.

The evidence suggests that the median renter was better housed at a lower rent in 1980 than in 1970, but that the median landlord was less well off. Median rents did not keep pace with the consumer price index or the cost of operating rental property. Between 1970 and 1980, the CPI for fuel and utility prices increased by 160.8 percent and the index for maintenance and repair costs by 130.9 percent. As a result landlords faced a squeeze in their profit margin. Over the decade they responded as might be expected: if their cash flow turned negative, they simply abandoned their properties; they became increasingly reluctant to develop new properties; and they became increasingly interested in converting rental properties to condominiums or cooperatives.

It is difficult to explain precisely why real rents fell during the 1970s given the entry of the baby-boom generation into the housing market.[7] Many would have expected that the influx of young households, which have a high propensity to rent, would have put increasing pressure on the rental market and driven up real rents. The experience was the opposite. Still, real rents are expected to rise over the next decade to give landlords the incentive to maintain existing properties and to add to the stock of rental properties. This forecast of rising real rents implies increasing conflicts between landlords and tenants and continued public debate on policies such as rent control and condominium conversion.

Regional Housing Markets

The problem with analyzing national statistics is that there is not a "national" market. National statistics are an aggregate of results of thousands of individual regional markets. This section examines the relationship between the particular circumstances of small market areas and changes in housing cost and structure characteristics.

Identifying Regional Market Conditions

As Table 5.5 shows, the number of households in the United States grew between 1970 and 1980 by 16.7 million or 26.6 percent, of which the West and South captured 68 percent. Bydivision, the Middle Atlantic experienced the slowest growth, while the most rapid growth occurred in the Mountain division; increases in the Pacific, West South Central, East South Central, and South Atlantic divisions were also significant.

Within each of the nine census divisions, however, substantial differences appear. It has already been noted that central-city growth was much lower than suburban growth; that small cities grew much faster than larger metropolitan areas; and that non-metropolitan areas showed the highest growth rates of all regions of the country. To analyze the effect of these different growth rates on the use and characteristics of the housing stock, it is therefore necessary to disaggregate the data.[8]

In the discussion below, counties are used as the primary geographical unit. Counties or their equivalent exist in every state and the data are available for fixed areas over time. The analysis here categorizes all counties as either urban or rural, depending on whether more than half the population lived in areas classified as rural by the census in 1970 and 1980. Although this definition ignores the rural part of a predominantly urban county and the urban part of a predominantly rural county, such "minority" populations are likely to reflect the overall urban or rural character of the counties to which they belong.

Table 5.5

HOUSEHOLD GROWTH BY CENSUS DIVISION
(in thousands)

Division	Households		Change	
	1970	1980	Number	Percentage
Northeast				
New England	3,645	4,362	717	19.7
Middle Atlantic	11,837	13,109	1,272	10.1
North Central				
East North Central	12,383	14,054	2,271	18.3
West North Central	5,150	6,200	1,050	20.4
West				
Mountain	2,518	3,986	1,468	58.3
Pacific	8,574	11,456	2,882	33.6
South				
West South Central	5,948	8,276	2,328	39.1
East South Central	3,865	5,051	1,186	30.7
South Atlantic	9,015	12,575	3,560	39.5
TOTAL	62,937	79,668	16,731	26.6

Regional figures may not add up to totals due to rounding.

SOURCE: Joint Center tabulations of Census of Population and Housing, 1970: First Count Summary Tapes; and Census of Population and Housing, 1980: Summary Tape File 1C (Washington, DC: U.S. Government Printing Office).

Moreover, few of the more than 3,000 counties in the United
States contain such an even mixture of urban and rural
population that they cannot safely be categorized as one or
the other.

The statistics in Table 5.6 indicate that household
growth in the 1970s nationwide was 24.8 percent in urban
counties compared with 33.3 percent in rural counties.   In
the Pacific division, urban counties grew substantially
more slowly than rural counties; in the Mountain region,
however, urban counties showed a higher household growth
rate than rural counties.   In parts of the country experiencing overall slower growth (New England, Middle Atlantic,
East North Central), rural counties grew faster.

Table 5.7 divides the counties into three groups according to the rate of household growth over the 1970s.
The slow-growth category of 114 counties represented one-
quarter of all households in 1970.   The most rapid growth
of any of these counties was 12 percent over the decade.
The medium-growth group comprises enough counties to include half of all households in 1970.   These counties experienced growth between 12 and 36 percent.   Finally, the
fast-growth group of counties contained the remaining
one-quarter of 1970 households.   The 266 counties in the
fast-growth group all had growth rates of more than 37
percent.

The same number of households, 25 percent of the total,
was represented in 266 fast-growth counties and only 114
slow-growth counties.   This indicates that fast-growth
counties had fewer households and slow-growth counties had
more households on average.   The smaller, fast-growth
counties, beginning with 25 percent of the 1970 households,
captured 58 percent of household growth to end with 31
percent of the 1980 households.   In contrast, the larger,
slow-growth counties, which began with roughly the same
number of 1970 households, accounted for only 3.3 percent
of total household growth, ending with 21 percent of the
1980 households.

Fast-Growth Areas.   A majority (53.4 percent) of new
housing units added during the 1970s were located in the
266 fast-growth counties.   While Table 5.8 shows that rapid
growth was concentrated primarily in southern and western
divisions, pockets of intense activity existed in all sections of the country including rural and suburban sections
of the East and North Central divisions.

Table 5.6

HOUSEHOLD GROWTH BY DIVISION AND URBAN AND RURAL COUNTIES, 1970–1980

(thousands of households)

Division	Urban Counties				Rural Counties			
	Number of Counties	1970 Households	Household Growth Thousands	%	Number of Counties	1970 Households	Household Growth Thousands	%
New England	30	3,141	535	17.0	37	505	182	36.0
Middle Atlantic	70	10,373	901	8.7	80	1,465	369	25.2
East North Central	136	9,863	1,564	15.9	301	2,520	707	28.1
West North Central	159	3,453	711	20.6	457	1,697	338	19.9
Mountain	106	2,098	1,242	59.2	173	420	226	53.7
Pacific	66	8,056	2,592	32.2	71	516	290	56.1
West South Central	189	4,638	1,848	39.8	281	1,310	480	36.6
East South Central	66	2,165	615	28.4	298	1,700	571	33.6
South Atlantic	132	6,006	2,341	39.0	437	3,010	1,218	40.5
TOTAL	954	49,795	12,350	24.8	2,136	13,142	4,381	33.3

Regional figures may not add up to totals due to rounding.

SOURCE: Joint Center tabulations of Census of Population and Housing, 1970: First Count Summary Tapes; and Census of Population and Housing, 1980: Summary Tape File 1C (Washington, DC: U.S. Government Printing Office).

Table 5.7

HOUSEHOLD GROWTH BY COUNTY GROWTH RATE, 1970-1980

Counties	Percentage of all Counties	1970 Households (1000s)	%	1980 Households (1000s)	%	Share of Growth (%) 1970-80
Slow-growth	16.9	15,814	25	16,344	21	3.2
Medium-growth	55.2	31,646	50	38,925	49	43.5
Fast-growth	27.9	15,477	25	24,409	31	53.4
TOTAL	100.0	62,937	100	79,678	100	100.0

SOURCE: Tabulations of Census of Population and Housing, 1970: First Count Summary Tapes; and Census of Population and Housing, 1980: Summary Tape File 1C (Cambridge, MA: Joint Center).

While the overwhelming majority of housing development occurred in urban counties, rural areas in all regions of the country grew at rates exceeding the national average: the rural growth for the decade was the largest percentage increase in the century. Equally significant is the fact that for the first time since the decade 1810-1820, housing in rural counties expanded more quickly than in urban counties. In the 1970s, rural housing units increased by more than in the preceding 30 years combined.

Taken collectively, non-metropolitan areas account for an important share of national housing market activity. The data in Table 5.9 show that 29.0 percent of total housing inventory growth in the 1970s occurred in non-metropolitan areas, nearly the same as the share in the 34 largest metropolitan areas.

The phenomenon of rural growth is not simply growth on the fringes of metropolitan areas. Counties not adjacent to metropolitan areas, with no settlement larger than 2,500 inhabitants, grew faster on the whole than metropolitan counties. Because the existing stock in rural areas is

Table 5.8

HOUSING UNIT GROWTH BY DIVISION, URBAN AND
RURAL COUNTIES, AND HOUSEHOLD GROWTH RATES, 1970–1980
(in thousands)

Division	Urban Counties			Rural Counties			Total
	Slow	Medium	Fast	Slow	Medium	Fast	
New England	62	448	85	0	116	108	819
Middle Atlantic	259	830	82	10	366	76	1,623
East North Central	370	1,162	258	15	549	294	2,648
West North Central	21	546	219	53	220	141	1,200
Mountain	6	113	1,324	6	38	284	1,771
Pacific	6	764	2,078	1	51	308	3,208
West South Central	30	689	1,350	3	200	377	2,649
East South Central	5	496	172	2	311	309	1,315
South Atlantic	17	694	2,092	2	571	893	4,269
TOTAL	776	5,742	7,660	92	2,422	2,810	19,502

SOURCE: Joint Center tabulations of Census of Population and Housing, 1970:
First Count Summary Tapes; and Census of Population and Housing, 1980: Summary Tape
File 1C (Washington, DC: U.S. Government Printing Office).

Table 5.9

HOUSING UNIT GROWTH BY TYPE OF PLACE, 1970–1980
(as percentage of total growth)

Type of Place	Central City	Suburb	Non–SMSA	Total
Non–SMSA	--	--	29.0	29.0
Small SMSA	5.5	9.1	--	14.6
Medium SMSA	7.5	18.3	--	25.8
Large SMSA	4.4	26.3	--	30.7
TOTAL	17.4	53.7	29.0	100.0

Figures are precentages of total growth.

NOTE: The 34 large SMSAs each had 1970 populations of 1 million or more. The 102 medium SMSAs had 1970 populations of from 250,000 to 1 million, while the 182 small SMSAs had 1970 populations of less than 250,000 (SMSAs as defined by the Office of Management and Budget as of June 30, 1981).

SOURCE: U.S. Bureau of the Census, Census of Population, Standard Metropolitan Statistical Areas and Standard Consolidated Areas–1980 (supplementary reports PC80–51–5 (Washington, DC: U.S. Government Printing Office).

small, households wishing to improve their housing situation must rely on new construction rather than upgrading through relocation.

In summary, most of the increment to the housing stock in the fast-growth counties occurred in the West and the South. The South Atlantic and Pacific regions captured 28 and 23 percent respectively of the total growth in fast-growth counties. Further, the West South Central and the Mountain regions each accounted for about 15 percent of the growth, leaving 19 percent for the other five regions. The non-metropolitan counties produced a significant part of the growth of fast-growth counties.

Slow-Growth Areas.   The slow-growth counties accounted for only four percent of housing unit additions.   Slow-growth areas ranged from central-city counties to rural counties where economic development has not occurred. Since the large cities in the Northeast have been losing population since 1950, one-third of the slow-growth urban counties are located in this region.   Some cities in southern and western counties also grew slowly in the 1970s. Typically, though, in all sections of the country, the suburban areas continued to grow even as the central cities declined.

Slow-growing rural areas experienced real stagnation, contributing less than two percent of the total rural housing development.   These counties are concentrated primarily in the Midwest and are often pockets of extreme poverty.

Local Market Outcomes of Growth Rates

Housing Values and Rents.   Housing value and rent changes are the most comprehensive summary measure of housing market changes.   The Census Bureau does not compile a rent index, but it does publish a distribution of values for owner-occupied units and a distribution of rents for renter-occupied units, including a mean for each.   The most serious shortcoming of these figures is that they are not adjusted for changes in the quality of housing through upgrading.   Thus, since changes in price cannot be distinguished from changes in quality,   only superficial analysis of value and rent changes is possible.

With these limitations in mind, Table 5.10 was compiled to present mean home values and mean rents for each of the county groupings.   For the nation as a whole, the mean home value increased by 186 percent and the mean rent by 108 percent over the 1970s.   There were systematic differences in these changes across the county groupings.   As would be expected, the fast-growth counties, which were under the most development pressure, experienced the largest increases in home values and rents, 15 to 20 percent greater than the mean.   By contrast, the slow-growth counties had from 10 to 20 percent smaller increases.

These general patterns hold true for both rural and urban counties, but the rate of change is greater in rural counties in nearly every category.   This difference reflects the substantially lower rents and home values of the rural counties at the beginning of the decade.   While part

Table 5.10

MEAN HOME VALUES AND RENTS BY URBAN AND RURAL
COUNTIES AND HOUSEHOLD GROWTH RATE, 1970-1980

Counties Growth Rate	Mean Home Value			Mean Rent		
	1970	1980	Increase (%)	1970	1980	Increase (%)
Urban						
Slow	$22,100	$53,200	141	108	212	95
Medium	20,600	57,900	182	103	213	106
Fast	20,500	67,700	229	108	237	120
Total	20,900	59,900	186	106	219	106
Rural						
Slow	10,400	29,800	138	53	110	106
Medium	13,300	37,800	183	62	137	121
Fast	14,900	47,700	220	68	168	148
Total	13,600	40,900	201	63	147	132
Total						
Slow	21,200	51,300	142	107	209	95
Medium	18,900	52,900	180	97	201	108
Fast	19,200	62,600	226	101	226	124
TOTAL	19,400	55,700	186	101	210	108

SOURCE: Joint Center tabulations of Census of Population
and Housing, 1970: First Count Summary Tapes; and Census
of Population and Housing, 1980: Summary Tape File 1C
(Washington, DC: U.S. Government Printing Office).

of the gain reflects an improvement in the quality of rural
units relative to urban units, a full equalization is
unlikely due to differences in land prices.

Homeownership. The comparison of growth rates in homeownership presented in Table 5.11 suggests very different
housing market circumstances across the county groupings.
The rural counties began the decade with a substantially
higher ownership rate (72.4 percent versus 60.4 percent)
and experienced stronger growth in homeownership (2.9
percent versus 1.0 percent) than did urban counties.

In the 1970s homeownership increased more in slow-
growth counties than in fast-growth counties, particularly
urban counties. In the slow-growth areas, the number of
owner households rose six percent while the number of
renter households decreased slightly. In these slow-growth
areas, the increases in income and wealth over the decade,
combined with demographic trends and low housing market
pressure, provided an opportunity for renter households to
make the transition to owning.

In fast-growth urban counties, in contrast, the number
of both owning and renting households increased substantially; the number of owning households rose nearly 57
percent, while an influx of young migrant households, with
a much higher propensity to rent, raised the number of
renting households by almost 60 percent. Together, these
trends induced only a small increase in the overall homeownership rate.

The fast-growth rural areas experienced a large influx
of family households with a much higher propensity for
single-family living and homeownership. Owning households
grew by 64 percent in these fast-growth rural counties
without an offsetting growth in renting households. As a
result, these counties posted a substantial increase of 3.2
percent in the ownership rate.

Housing Construction. Table 5.12 presents growth in
housing units according to structure type. Nationwide,
structures with two to nine units grew only by 1.2 percent
and decreased from 17.5 to 13.8 percent of the total stock.
Mobile homes, in contrast, grew by 135 percent and increased from 2.7 to 5.0 percent of the stock. Together,
single-family and mobile homes increased their share from
72.1 to 76.1 percent of the total housing stock.

The pattern of growth in all fast-growth and in rural
slow-growth counties mirrors the national trends. Mobile
homes grew faster than total units and increased as a

Table 5.11

CHANGES IN RATES OF HOMEOWNERSHIP AND RENTING BY URBAN
AND RURAL COUNTIES AND HOUSEHOLD GROWTH RATE, 1970-1980

Counties Growth Rate	Homeownership Rate (%)			Rates of Growth of Households (%)		
	1970	1980	Change	Owners	Renters	Total
Urban						
Slow	50.2	51.7	1.4	6.0	0.2	3.1
Medium	64.3	64.2	−0.1	6.0	0.2	3.1
Fast	65.4	65.0	−0.3	57.2	59.6	58.0
Total	60.4	61.4	1.0	26.9	21.6	24.8
Rural						
Slow	71.9	74.9	3.0	11.2	−4.8	6.7
Medium	72.3	74.9	2.6	29.6	13.2	25.1
Fast	72.8	76.0	3.2	64.1	38.8	57.3
Total	72.4	75.3	2.9	38.6	18.3	33.3
Total						
Slow	51.7	53.2	1.6	6.3	−0.2	3.2
Medium	66.3	67.9	0.7	24.2	20.4	22.9
Fast	67.3	67.8	0.6	59.1	55.2	57.8
TOTAL	62.9	64.4	1.6	29.7	21.2	26.5

SOURCE: Joint Center tabulations of Census of Population
and Housing, 1970: First Count Summary Tapes; and Census of
Population and Housing, 1980: Summary Tape File 1C (Washington, DC: U.S. Government Printing Office).

Table 5.12

GROWTH IN HOUSING UNITS BY STRUCTURE TYPE, URBAN AND RURAL COUNTIES, AND HOUSEHOLD GROWTH RATE, 1970-1980

Growth	1 Unit		2-9 Units		10+ Units		Mobile Homes		Total Housing
	1970-80 Growth (%)	Percentage of 1980 Inventory	1970-80 Growth (%)	Percentage of 1980 Inventory	1970-80 Growth (%)	Percentage of 1980 Inventory	1970-80 Growth (%)	Percentage of 1980 Inventory	Growth (%)
Urban	33.7	68.6	-1.6	15.5	20.6	12.3	110.3	3.6	24.8
Slow	19.8	53.9	-11.1	26.2	-6.2	19.0	46.4	1.0	3.1
Medium	27.7	74.2	-4.7	13.3	22.4	9.3	93.0	3.2	22.2
Fast	56.2	71.9	38.1	10.3	90.1	11.5	140.0	6.3	58.0
Rural	24.7	79.6	24.5	8.0	134.2	2.3	174.8	9.8	33.3
Slow	1.5	85.3	18.0	7.3	86.1	1.6	114.8	5.9	6.7
Medium	18.5	80.6	12.3	8.5	98.3	2.0	148.3	8.8	25.1
Fast	43.4	77.6	57.2	7.4	52.1	2.9	221.7	12.1	57.3
Total	31.3	71.1	1.2	13.8	23.7	10.1	134.8	5.0	26.5
Slow	17.5	56.1	-10.6	24.8	-5.9	17.8	63.4	1.3	3.2
Medium	24.9	75.9	-1.9	12.0	25.9	7.3	117.3	4.7	22.9
Fast	52.4	73.4	41.6	9.5	96.1	9.3	167.5	7.8	57.8

SOURCE: Joint Center tabulations of Census of Population and Housing, 1970: First Count Summary Tapes; and Census of Population and Housing, 1980: Summary Tape File 1C (Washington, DC: U.S. Government Printing Office).

percentage of the total inventory. Together, single-family and mobile homes roughly maintained their share of total units in these areas.

Urban slow-growth counties experienced a different pattern. In these counties, single-family and mobile homes increased from 50.9 to 57.4 percent of the housing stock. In our view, the decline in the share of multiple-family units in these areas reflects the important role of losses to the inventory in determining the changing composition of the housing stock. In the slow-growth urban counties, multi-family units (especially small structures, the oldest and least economical type) are being removed from the stock. Even with only modest growth, single-family and mobile homes have therefore increased as a percentage of the housing inventory in these counties.

This analysis of housing stock changes suggests that additions dominate changes in fast-growth counties while losses are more important in slow-growth counties. Both new construction and removals reflect the operation of the market as demand and supply are equilibrated. The outcome of this process depends on the characteristics of households and the characteristics of the existing stock.

NOTES

1. This section draws on H. James Brown, Karl Case, and Kermit Baker, "Homeownership and Housing Affordability in the United States, 1963-1983" (Cambridge, MA: Joint Center for Urban Studies, 1983).

2. Federal National Mortgage Association, "Housing Finance in the 1980s: Issues and Options" (FNMA Symposium, February 1981); and Karl Case, "Land Prices, Housing Prices and Housing Production: Does the Housing Market Work or Doesn't It?" (paper prepared for Joint Center for Urban Studies/ Lincoln Institute of Land Policy conference, March 1982).

3. For two excellent reviews of this issue, see Kermit Baker, "Housing Affordability" (Ph.D. dissertation, Massachusetts Institute of Technology, 1983); and John Tuccillo, Housing and Investment in an Inflationary World: Theory and Evidence (Washington, DC: The Urban Institute, 1980).

4. Case, "Land Prices"; and Gary Hack and Otis Ginoza, "Private and Public Responsibilities in Housing Site Development" (Cambridge, MA: Joint Center for Urban Studies, 1982). See also Urban Systems Research and Engineering, Economic Impact of Environmental Regulations on Housing (Cambridge, MA, 1981); and results of a study of the U.S. Task Force on Housing Costs (Washington, DC: U.S. Department of Housing and Urban Development, 1978).

5. The Report of The President's Commission on Housing (Washington, DC: U.S. Government Printing Office, 1983).

6. Ira S. Lowry, "Inflation Indexes for Rental Housing," N-1832-HUD, (Santa Monica, CA: Rand Corporation, 1982).

7. Ira S. Lowry, "Rental Housing in the 1970s: Searching for the Crisis," in Rental Housing: Is There A Crisis?, edited by John C. Weicher, Kevin Villani, and Elizabeth Roistacher (Washington, DC: The Urban Institute, 1981); and Robyn Swaim Phillips, "Explaining the Decline in Real Residential Rents, 1970-1980: The Rental Housing Crisis Reconsidered" (Ph.D. dissertation, Harvard University, 1983).

8. We were unable to adjust the census data used in the disaggregated analysis for undercount problems. Using unadjusted data should not, however, affect analysis of the location of growth or estimation of relative growth rates.

6

REVIEW OF
HOUSING MARKET FORECASTS

Between 1975 and 1979, a series of housing market forecasts predicted that the aging of the baby-boom generation
as well as the continuing need to upgrade the existing
housing stock would spark record-level new construction
activity in the 1980s. Researchers at the U.S. Forest
Service, the Urban Institute, the National Association of
Home Builders, and Data Resources, Inc., among others,
published projections that new construction would add 24 to
28 million units to the housing stock over the decade.[1]
When the economy sank into deep recession in the early
1980s, many forecasting groups reduced their estimates of
total production. It is not likely, however, that the
revised predictions are more accurate than those they
replaced: like earlier estimates, the more recent housing
market forecasts fail to capture how demographic factors
influence patterns of demand and, in particular, household
growth. In addition, they do not consider factors that
influence losses, conversions, and other forms of housing
investment and disinvestment. Although existing models may
forecast total housing market activity accurately, they are
unable to identify important trends in the distribution of
new construction by location, size, or structure type.

Selected Forecasts

Forecasts of housing consumption and investment activity require an understanding of the way in which both

households and the housing stock adjust to changing economic conditions. New construction contributes only a
small addition each year to the total housing inventory.
Even after a decade of record-level new construction activity, four of every five U.S. households in 1980 lived in a
unit that had been built before 1970. The location, quality, and other characteristics of the current inventory
thus play an important, although frequently ignored, role
in shaping housing market trends.

Demographic characteristics and household formation
patterns also influence housing market behavior. The
formation of new households and the composition of existing
households depend not only on economic factors governing
the cost and availability of housing, but also on social
norms such as marriage rates, divorce rates, and the age at
which children leave their parents' homes. Like the characteristics of the existing housing stock, the current
characteristics of families and households have important
implications for the future.

In attempting to capture the many economic and social
factors that influence housing investment and consumption
decisions, housing analysts employ a variety of techniques
ranging from simple trend-line extrapolations to complex
simultaneous equation models. The work of the ten forecasting groups listed in Table 6.1 illustrates this
diversity. Researchers at Data Resources, Inc. (DRI), for
example, employ one of the largest and most complex macroeconomic models of the national economy in use today, yet
supplement the results of this model with simple trend-line
forecasts. The same is true for Morgan Stanley and Com-
pany, whose housing forecasts are based in part on the
results of the national macroeconomic model of Townsend
Greenspan, Inc. and in part on supplementary analyses of
factors not included in the national model.

Although it is useful to think about housing in the
context of the national economy, macroeconomic models
typically contain only limited detail about the housing
sector. The DRI model, for example, forecasts single-
family and multi-family housing starts and mobile home
placements for the next 25 years, but not the number and
composition of households living in these units. To
supplement their national models, analysts at DRI and
elsewhere have therefore developed special housing sector
models. The Regional Data Associates model, initially
developed by Kenneth Rosen and Dwight Jaffee, is an example

Table 6.1

SELECTED HOUSING MARKET FORECASTS

Forecasting Group	Recent Publications
Advance Mortgage Corporation	"U.S. Housing Markets," July 31, 1981.
Data Resources, Inc.	"Realities of Long-run Housing Demand," Data Resources U.S. Long-Term Review, Fall 1981.
Anthony Downs	Search for Space: Rental Housing in the 1980s, draft report, Summer 1982.
Thomas C. Marcin, Forest Products Laboratory	"Outlook for Housing by Type of Unit and Region: 1978 to 2020," USDA Forest Service Research Paper, 1977.
Morgan Stanley and Company	"Outlook for Timber Supply/ Demand through 1990," text of speech delivered by Thomas P. Clephawe to Workshop on Financing Forestry Investment, Duke University, May 10, 1982.
National Association of Homebuilders	"The Eighties: After a Slow Start, Some Very Good Years," Builder, January 7, 1980.
Regional Data Associates/ Kenneth Rosen and Dwight Jaffee, University of California, Berkeley Princeton University	"The Demand for Housing and Mortgage Credit: The Mortgage Credit Gap Problem," paper prepared for FNMA Symposium on Housing Finance in the Eighties, February 1981.
George Sternlieb and James W. Hughes, Rutgers University	"Housing: Past and Future," paper prepared for FNMA Symposium on Housing Finance in the Eighties, February 1981.
John Weicher, Lorene Yap, and Mary Jones, The Urban Institute	Metropolitan Housing Needs for the 1980s (Washington, D.C.: The Urban Institute, 1982).
U.S. Bureau of the Census	"Projections of the Number of Households and Families: 1978- 1995," Current Population Reports, P-25, May 1979.

SOURCE: Compiled by the authors.

of this type, as are the models of Thomas Marcin of the
U.S. Forest Service, John Weicher of the Urban Institute,
and researchers at Advance Mortgage Corporation.

While assuming certain parameters about the future of
the national economy, each model nonetheless emphasizes
different aspects of the housing market. The most recent
version of the RDA/Rosen/Jaffee model, for instance, incorporates considerable detail about housing finance and
includes a simple model of household formation, but treats
as exogenous the rates of net loss to the existing inventory.[2]   In contrast, Weicher does not attempt to model
household formation but uses the available Census Bureau
forecasts; he focuses instead on modeling the components of
inventory change, including losses.   Marcin pays more
attention to the details of the household formation process
than RDA/Rosen/Jaffe, but less attention than Weicher to
the details of housing inventory adjustment.

In addition to these formal models, many analysts make
qualitative assessments of the future of the housing industry. As part of the multi-year study on urban decline and
the future of the U.S. city, Anthony Downs of the Brookings
Institution has developed estimates of likely trends in
housing construction and investment.   Downs combines the
Census Bureau forecasts of household formation with independent economic analyses of inventory adjustment to form
alternative forecasts of housing market activities. George
Sternlieb takes a similar approach in his work on multi-
family housing demand.   Without the benefit of formal
models (or perhaps because they were not bound to the
limitations of a single model), both Downs and Sternlieb
offer far-ranging and frequently insightful comments about
future housing market dynamics.

To varying degrees, housing market forecasters seek to
assess the demographic, economic, technological, social,
and political factors that affect housing consumption and
investment. While it is of course difficult to develop a
single model that incorporates all of these complex inter-
actions, current forecasting efforts seem most deficient in
tracking changes in demographic patterns and in the use of
the existing inventory. The next section assesses alternative forecasts of household formation, and the section
after evaluates forecasts of the components of inventory
change. This review suggests that existing projections of
housing market activity are built on tenuous foundation.

Forecasts of Household Formation

The 1970s recorded unusually rapid growth in the number
of households and a marked shift in household composition.
Over the decade, the number of households increased by 16.8
million, compared with 10.6 million in each of the previous
two decades. While forecasters expected the <u>number</u> of
households to increase significantly with the arrival of
the baby-boom generation in the prime household formation
age groups, many analysts, including those at the Census
Bureau, failed to anticipate the rapid growth in household
headship <u>rates</u>.   With higher incomes and more generous
federal housing programs, more individuals were able to
maintain independent households.   When actual household
growth in the 1970s exceeded expectations, the Census
Bureau revised upward its projections for the 1980s.   The
1979 revision estimated that the number of households will
increase by 13.0 to 18.8 million between 1980 and 1990,
with the most likely estimate being 16.8 million.

A dramatic change also occurred in the composition of
families and households during the 1970s.   As Chapter 2
notes, married couples accounted for almost 80 percent of
all households in 1950 and over 60 percent of new households added during that decade.   Since 1970, however,
married couples have constituted a continually smaller
share of total households as more couples delay marriage,
get divorced, or simply live together.   As Figure 6.1
illustrates, the number of married-couple households increased by only 250,000 each year between 1975 and 1980,
compared with an annual growth of all households of 1.6
million.   As a result, married couples accounted for less
than 15 percent of total household growth during this
period, the lowest share ever recorded.

Despite these trends, the Census Bureau's projections
for the 1980s imply a resurgence in married-couple households above the levels observed in the 1970s, and that
families other than married couples will continue to grow
at approximately the same rates as in the past decade.
There is little reason to expect, however, that marriage
rates will increase.   Since "other families" consist primarily of single women with children, continued growth in
this group would require illegitimate births to increase
above 1970s levels and divorces to involve more women with
children.   With fertility stable or declining, neither of
these increases is likely.

Figure 6.1

ANNUAL INCREASE IN NUMBER OF HOUSEHOLDS
BY TYPE, 1950–1980

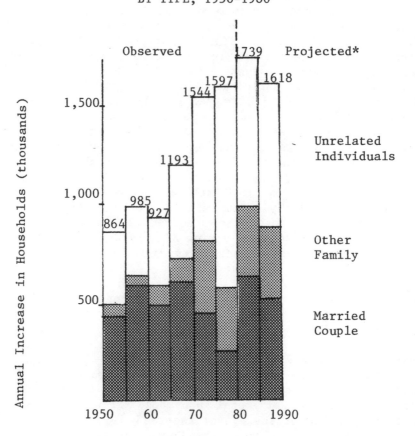

* Census Bureau Series B.

SOURCES: U.S. Bureau of the Census, Current
Population Reports (series P-20, nos. 345 and 366;
series P-25, no. 805) (Washington, DC: U.S. Government Printing Office, 1980).

Examination of the Census Bureau's forecasting methodology suggests the source of these errors. Using data for
the period 1964-1978, Census Bureau analysts first projected total population by age and sex assuming the continuation of observed trends in births, deaths, and net
immigration to the country, and then calculated the share
of persons of a given age in a particular marital status
for each year. After fitting a series of nonlinear equations to the time trends in these shares, they used these
equations to project future distributions of population by
marital status. Also using simple extrapolation procedures, the Census Bureau analysts estimated the probability
that an individual of given age and marital status would
head a household.

In 1979, the Joint Center presented forecasts demon-
strating that the widely used census projection of 16.8
million new households for the 1980s was between 2.0 and
3.0 million too high. Nevertheless, other housing market
analysts have continued to use the Census Bureau predictions of household growth. For example, recent work by the
Advance Mortgage Corporation and George Sternlieb incorporates the census projections without change; Anthony Downs
and John Weicher have also used census forecasts as input,
with only minor modifications. Each of these analyses not
only overstates the probable growth in total households but
also presents an inaccurate view of the growth of households headed by individuals of a particular age or marital
status.

Although Marcin, Data Resources, and RDA/Rosen/Jaffee
have developed economic analyses of household formation,
their projections are unlikely to improve on those of the
Census Bureau, especially as they relate to household
formation among specific age groups. DRI fits a simple
time trend-line to age-specific headship rates using data
for the past 30 years. Since annual average headship rates
grew more slowly between 1950 and 1980 than between 1964
and 1978, the DRI projections of household growth are lower
than Census Bureau forecasts.

Using a slightly different procedure, Thomas Marcin
calculates a theoretical maximum headship rate for each age
group based on estimated growth in the number of married
couples. Marcin then correlates annual estimates of age-
specific headship for the period 1953-1976 to annual
estimates of per capita income, and in essence forces the
trend-line to approach asymptotically the maximum headship
rate. Based on these equations, Marcin generates two sets

of estimates of household growth assuming a 1.0 and a 2.0 percent growth in income. Like those of Data Resources, Marcin's estimates of household growth are lower than the Census Bureau's, largely due to his assumptions about maximum headship rates.

RDA/Rosen/Jaffee treat household formation as one of the demand factors in a simultaneous equation model of housing supply and demand. The key variables influencing household headship are real disposable income, the cost of maintaining a separate housing unit (as proxied by the rental and homeownership component of the consumer price index), and the unemployment rate. RDA/Rosen/Jaffee estimate separate equations for two household types (family and nonfamily) in each of four age groups (15-24, 25-34, 35-64, and 65+). The number of families with a head aged 65+ is a function of the total number of people aged 65+, income growth, and the homeownership component of the CPI. The number of households aged 35-64 depends, in turn, on the total number of people aged 35-64, the cost of housing, the marriage rate, and the divorce rate.[3]

While household formation appears to be fully endogenous to the RDA/Rosen/Jaffee model, this is more in principle than in fact. Although RDA/Rosen/Jaffee argue forcefully that household formation depends on both economic and social factors, social factors (proxied by marriage and divorce rates) appear in only three of the eight household equations. Marriage and divorce rates thus influence the growth of family households aged 35-64, while the divorce rate influences the growth of nonfamily households aged 25-34 and 35-64. For the five other groups, RDA/Rosen/Jaffee apparently did not find statistically significant models that included marriage rates, divorce rates, and other factors of the probability that a given age group would form households. Indeed, for the group aged 15-24, headship depends only on the growth of income and change in total CPI, two factors that are exogenously specified. As a result, the age group with the greatest potential to change its headship rate is, in fact, not formally represented in the simultaneously determined market process.

The comparison presented in Table 6.2 illustrates how different assumptions about household formation affect age-specific household forecasts. For example, the Census Bureau predicts a slight growth in the number of households aged 14-24, while Data Resources and Marcin both predict declines. Assuming that income grows by one percent per

Table 6.2

COMPARISON OF AGE-SPECIFIC HOUSEHOLD FORECASTS, 1980-1990
(in thousands)

Forecaster	Age of Household Head				Total
	14-24	25-34	35-64	65+	
U.S. Census Bureau, series 2B (1979)	77	4,420	8,441	3,838	16,783
Data Résources (Fall 1981)	-320	3,115	7,925	3,580	14,300
Thomas Marcin (1977)					
High	-339	3,661	7,937	3,322	14,580
Low	-619	3,141	7,655	3,144	13,319
RDA/Rosen/Jaffe (May 1982)					
Optimistic	704	5,356	8,766	4,334	19,160
Base	432	4,388	8,210	3,625	16,656
Pessimistic	-46	3,705	7,437	2,536	12,632

Figures may not add up to totals due to rounding.

NOTE: Thomas Marcin forecasts for households 18 years of age and older. Data Resources, Inc. forecasts for households 20 years of age and older.

SOURCE: See Table 6.1.

year, Marcin's "low series" projects a decrease of 619,000 in the number of households aged 18-25. It should be noted that the Marcin and DRI forecasts are quite close for each of the other age groups, suggesting that Marcin may have simply produced a somewhat more complex representation of the DRI time-trend.

RDA/Rosen/Jaffee predict, in contrast, that the number of young households will increase fairly significantly. Their three scenarios include a base forecast assuming a 1.7 percent growth rate in real per capita income and a 9.2 percent inflation rate; a more optimistic forecast assuming that real per capita income will grow at an annual average rate of 3.1 percent, with inflation averaging 6.5 percent for the decade; and a pessimistic forecast assuming that income will fall by 0.3 percent annually and inflation will surge ahead at 12.1 percent. Under baseline conditions, the RDA/Rosen/Jaffee model predicts that headship rates among the group aged 15-25 will continue to rise rapidly, a forecast that runs counter to the experience of the last seven years. Even in their most pessimistic scenario, the basic assumptions of which are extremely unlikely, the RDA/Rosen/Jaffee model forecasts a 20 percent increase in headship rates and only slight declines in the number of households under 25.

The RDA/Rosen/Jaffee, DRI, and Marcin models move directly from forecasting population by age to forecasting households by age without explicitly modeling the intervening step of family formation. The details of the family formation process, however, can and do influence the probability of living independently. Depending on economic factors such as income, relative housing prices, and unemployment levels, a given family nucleus may or may not form a household. Each of the models thus fails to represent fully the economic and demographic forces that shape future patterns of household formation. Rather than starting with a simple forecast of population by age, a model of headship rates and housing consumption should begin with a forecast of population by age, marital status, and presence or absence of children.

Forecasts of Inventory Change

In addition to overstating rates of household formation, current housing forecasts tend to overestimate likely net losses to the inventory. As Table 6.3 shows, only the

Table 6.3

COMPARISON OF ALTERNATIVE FORECASTS OF
INVENTORY CHANGE, 1980–1990
(thousands of units)

Forecaster	Change in Total Stock	Net Losses	New Construction Plus Mobile Home Placements
Advance Mortgage (July 1981)			
High	17,670	3,080	20,750
Low	13,550	4,200	17,750
Data Resources (Fall 1981)	15,845	4,320	20,165
Anthony Downs (1982)	15,540	4,560	20,100
Thomas Marcin (1977)			
High	16,185	9,068	25,253
Low	14,801	8,374	23,175
Morgan Stanley (May 1982)	na	na	18,890
RDA/Rosen/Jaffee (May 1982)			
Optimistic	18,840	5,060	23,900
Base	16,510	4,010	20,530
Pessimistic	11,870	2,490	14,360
John Weicher (1980)	18,786	7,956	26,742

na: not available.

SOURCE: See Table 6.1.

pessimistic scenario of the RDA/ Rosen/Jaffee model forecasts relatively low net losses. Interestingly enough, the
Advance Mortgage Corporation forecast seems to associate
slow growth in total households and in the housing stock
with reduced pressures to conserve the inventory, and thus
with higher net losses. RDA/Rosen/Jaffee argue, in contrast, that the high cost of new housing both slows household formation and encourages more intensive use of the
existing inventory.

With the exception of the Census Bureau, all the forecasters discussed here issue detailed projections of new
construction activity. Since Sternlieb limits his forecasts to the rental housing sector, and Weicher to housing
construction in metropolitan areas, their projections do
not appear in Table 6.4; also missing is the prediction of
Anthony Downs, who focuses on new construction of owner and
renter units. While estimates of total construction differ
considerably, the forecasters (with one notable exception)

Table 6.4

COMPARISON OF ALTERNATIVE FORECASTS
OF NEW CONSTRUCTION BY TYPE, 1980-1990

Forecast	Single-family	Multi-family	Mobile Homes	Total
Advance Mortgage				
High	NA	NA	2,500	20,750
Low	NA	NA	2,500	20,750
Date Resources (Fall 1981)	11,045	6,000	2,120	20,165
Thomas Marcin (1977)				
High	16,393	5,335	3,524	25,253
Low	15,249	4,706	3,220	23,175
Morgan Stanley (1982)	8,520	6,980	3,390	18,890
RDA/Rosen/Jaffee (May 1982)				
Optimistic	13,720	6,450	3,620	23,900
Base	12,200	5,250	2,070	20,530
Pessimistic	8,560	3,610	2,190	14,360

NA: not available.

SOURCE: See Table 6.1

generally agree that in the 1980s, the single-family share of conventional new construction (that is, excluding mobile homes) will be between 65 and 75 percent.

The Morgan Stanley forecast, prepared in consultation with Townsend-Greenspan, presents quite a different view. Reacting to record mortgage interest rates and what they see as the general disarray of the thrift industry, Morgan Stanley assumes that homeownership affordability problems will severely limit the demand for new single-family homes over the next ten years. As a result, they predict that the single-family share of conventional new construction will decline to roughly half by 1990. Although offering no exact figures, Sternlieb makes a similar assessment: new construction in the 1980s will be oriented less toward single-family homes and more toward townhouses and multi-family structures as consumers adapt their expectations to the realities of their limited purchasing power.

Whether single-family housing starts are 50 percent or 75 percent of total new construction, of course, makes a considerable difference to the housing industry. The Morgan Stanley report notes that a single-family home uses about twice as much lumber and plywood as multi-family units. There are equally important differences in the financing and construction of single- and multi-family structures. Differential rates of gross losses are also likely to influence the types of new construction. If loss rates among multi-family units continue to decline, con-struction levels for these units will also decrease. Moreover, conversions of single-family homes and adaptive reuse of commercial and industrial space can add signifi-cant numbers of units to the multi-family stock, thus depressing new construction.

Given the important link between use of the existing stock and new construction activity, there has been sur-prisingly little empirical research on the economic de-terminants of losses and other additions. Using Annual Housing Survey data for 59 metropolitan areas, Weicher found that loss rates between 1970 and 1976 were higher in areas with a large volume of new construction and lower in areas with high overall growth rates, particularly among areas with predominantly minority households. Weicher included measures of income growth, growth in the costs of new construction, and the amount of subsidized housing, but could find no statistically significant relationship between these variables and loss rates. Surprisingly, how-ever, he did not employ measures of the initial quality of

the housing inventory, a factor that would explain the high
loss rates in the Northeast and North Central regions of
the country. Nor did Weicher note the tendency for losses
to be related to the presence of mobile homes in an area.
Inclusion of these variables would likely increase the
explanatory power of the loss equation and perhaps lead to
a more understandable pattern of coefficients for the other
economic variables.

In his analysis of other additions, Weicher finds that
conversions are inversely related to the increase in small
families, a result that he notes is just the opposite of
what should be expected. Weicher concedes that the estimates of non-new construction for particular SMSAs are
likely to contain errors, but does not explore these
issues.

Given the difficulty of forming even a rough estimate
of non-new construction additions in the 1970s, forecasting
trends in this type of housing production is a perilous
exercise. Yet non-new construction additions are simply
too important too ignore: even the lower-bound estimate of
2.7 million other additions for the 1970s implies that this
source of inventory adjustment contributed more than twice
as many units as in the 1960s. Weicher estimates, however,
that non-new construction additions will equal only 1.2
million units, while Advance Mortgage predicts that they
will be as high as 5.9 million. DRI's estimate of 3.5
million units thus appears to be the most plausible.

Data problems limited the ability of the other forecasters to analyze fully the effect of changing patterns of
inventory losses and non-new construction, or other, additions. Marcin made no distinction between gross losses and
other additions but instead attempted to explain variation
in net losses over time and across regions as a function of
economic variables such as growth of income, capital cost,
housing prices, and housing operating costs. Marcin reported that net housing replacement is related to these
variables, but that his equations were highly unstable.

Since RDA/Rosen/Jaffee were also unable to develop
sound econometric estimates of the determinants of net loss
rates, they were forced to make the net loss rate exogenous
to their model. For each scenario, they therefore had to
determine a consistent net loss rate, that is, a range of
50 percent between the optimistic and pessimistic scenarios
of net losses, producing estimates for the decade from 5.0
to 2.5 million units. They could just as well have assumed
that losses do not respond as readily to economic changes

but rather are determined largely by the initial quality of the housing stock or by the rates of household growth by region. If under baseline economic conditions net losses hold at 2.6 million units, a level consistent with recent trends, the RDA/Rosen/Jaffee estimates of new construction are likely to be high.

The failure to represent net losses explicitly entails serious problems. Because they fail to model changing uses of the existing housing inventory, analyses of the relationship between economic climate and new construction activity are suspect. The changing patterns of losses and non-new construction additions are simply too important to ignore.

NOTES

1. For a review of the earlier housing forecasts, see John Weicher, Lorene Yap, and Mary S. Jones, Metropolitan Housing Needs for the 1980s (Washington, DC: The Urban Institute, 1982).

2. The Rosen/Jaffee model is now maintained by Regional Data Associates, a subsidiary of Chase Econometrics. This chapter refers to forecasts prepared by Kenneth Rosen in May 1982 for the National Association of Home Builders. These forecasts exhibit no substantial differences from those used to prepare the Rosen/Jaffee presentation to the FNMA Symposium in February 1981. For a more recent discussion of the RDA version of the model, see Chase Econometrics, RDA Quarterly Forecast Report (Bala Cynwyd, PA: 1983).

3. For a brief discussion of each of the sectors of the RDA/Rosen/Jaffee model, see Regional Data Associates material entitled "Overview of the Models."

7

OUTLOOK FOR THE 1980s

Projection of the number, type, and composition of households requires estimating changes in the variables discussed in Chapter 2, (i.e., changes in marital status, family composition, and rates of household headship). Our method of making these estimates is cohort analysis of trends among categories of household heads, or "family nuclei." Based on this analysis, the number of households is projected to grow at an average annual rate of 1.48 million in the 1980s.

Growth in the number of households plus changes in the number of vacant housing units equals change in the total housing inventory. Similarly, inventory change equals new construction activity (conventional new construction plus mobile home placements) less net losses (total losses less non-new construction additions). Our baseline projection is for an average annual increase in the total housing stock of 1.67 million units with new construction plus mobile home shipments averaging about 1.89 million.

Although household formation rates vary across regions, the broad trends in the nine census divisions tend to parallel those of the nation as a whole. Based on this consistency and estimated regional population growth, over 70 percent of the growth in households and new construction activity is projected to occur in the South and West.

National Projections

Population and Family Nuclei

The Joint Center's household projections are based on the national population projections summarized in Table 7.1. Although similar to the most recent census forecasts, these numbers are derived by a markedly different method. First, the Joint Center estimates are based on a single set of "best guess" assumptions about fertility, mortality, and immigration. The Census Bureau, however, publishes a series of alternative forecasts based on high, medium, and low estimates of these variables. Second, the Joint Center projections inflate the 1980 census data to compensate for estimated undercount. The Census Bureau's approach is to assume that the undercount in the 1980 data is negligible and to extrapolate directly from the 1980 census figures.[1] Finally, we make separate state-by-state projections and add them together to arrive at a national total. The census, by contrast, derives state population growth from an aggregated national forecast, and thus the state estimates are constrained by the national figure.

As Table 7.1 shows, the Joint Center projects a 1985 population that is 1.5 million greater than the census middle series; by the year 2000, this gap widens to over 5.5 million. Most of the difference is due to assuming higher levels of immigration, and higher fertility rates consistent with a greater proportion of foreign-born.

Unlike the Census Bureau, the Joint Center also produces projections for several household categories or "family nuclei." As described in Chapter 3, the behavior of a particular family nucleus (e.g., divorced women aged 25-29 with two children) is projected by following the household category over time as it ages.[2] For every five-year age group, our analysis employs 16 such categories broken down by sex, marital status, and presence of children under the age of 15:

Married couples with no children
Married couples with one child
Married couples with two or three children
Married couples with four or more children
Never married males
Previously married males with no children
Previously married males with children
Never married females with no children

Table 7.1

COMPARISON OF CENSUS (MIDDLE SERIES)
AND JOINT CENTER POPULATION PROJECTIONS
(in thousands)

Age Group	1985	1990	1995	2000
< 20				
Joint Center	71,810	74,220	77,126	79,879
Census Middle	70,247	71,532	73,685	74,851
Difference	1,563	2,688	3,441	5,028
20 - 24				
Joint Center	21,405	18,706	17,683	17,914
Census Middle	21,282	18,567	17,129	17,126
Difference	123	139	554	788
25 - 34				
Joint Center	42,085	44,258	41,524	37,822
Census Middle	41,781	43,506	40,489	36,387
Difference	304	752	1,035	1,435
35 - 49				
Joint Center	43,347	51,428	59,680	64,404
Census Middle	43,640	51,818	59,660	63,471
Difference	-293	-390	20	933
50 - 64				
Joint Center	33,071	32,158	33,891	39,965
Census Middle	33,026	32,508	34,663	41,120
Difference	45	-350	-772	-1,155
65+				
Joint Center	28,333	31,077	32,924	33,667
Census Middle	28,673	31,799	34,006	35,036
Difference	-340	-722	-1,082	-1,369
All Ages				
Joint Center	240,050	251,848	262,829	273,650
Census Middle	238,648	249,731	259,631	267,990
Difference	1,402	2,117	3,198	5,660

SOURCE: U.S. Bureau of the Census, _Projections of the Number of Households and Families: 1979-1995_ (Current Population Reports, P25) (Washington, DC: U.S. Government Printing Office.

Never married females with children

Divorced, separated, married/spouse absent females with no children

Divorced, separated, married/spouse absent females with one child

Divorced, separated, married/spouse absent females with two or three children

Divorced, separated, married/spouse absent females with four or more children

Widowed females with no children

Widowed females with one child

Widowed females with two or more children

This typology of families and individuals differs from the census definitions of households, families, and primary individuals; it is designed instead to account for all adult individuals and couples, whether presently heading a household or living with other adults, who could potentially form (head) a separate household without changing marital status. Defined in this way, the population of potential household heads or family nuclei consists of both families and individuals. Every household (except a negligible number having no members over age 14) includes at least one such family or individual. It should be noted that every member of the household population belongs to one and only one family nucleus.

Table 7.2 indicates that married couples constituted 51.6 percent of the family nuclei (74.7 percent of all households) in 1960. By 1980, the proportion of married-couple nuclei fell to 41.5 percent (60.5 percent of total households). This was caused by the baby-boom generation swelling the ranks of 20-34-year-olds but continuing to delay marriage. We predict that during the decade the proportion of married-couple nuclei will stabilize as the baby bust replaces the baby boom in these age groups, assuming that the younger generation maintains the same patterns of late marriage.

The aging of the baby-boom generation and the maturing of the baby-bust generation into young adulthood are the most significant demographic trends affecting potential household formation. By the middle of the decade, the baby-boom generation will have made its contribution to the number of new households. The delayed marriages of baby-boom cohorts now in their late twenties and thirties have, in fact, begun to reduce the number of households: once headship rates among the unmarried exceed 50 percent,

Table 7.2

DISTRIBUTION OF FAMILY NUCLEI, 1960–1990

Household Type	1960	1970	1980	Projected 1990
Married Couples				
No Children under 15 Present	23.1	23.0	22.6	20.1
Children under 15 Present	28.5	23.9	18.9	20.9
Other Male Head				
Never-Married	15.0	16.5	19.2	17.7
Previously Married				
No Children under 15 Present	5.4	5.3	6.0	6.9
Children under 15 Present	0.4	0.6	0.5	0.7
Other Female Head				
Never-Married				
No Children under 15 Present	12.5	14.3	15.7	14.3
Children under 15 Present	0.2	0.5	1.0	1.0
Divorced/Separated				
No Children under 15 Present	3.2	3.9	4.5	5.1
Children under 15 Present	2.0	2.4	3.2	3.9
Widowed				
No Children under 15 Present	8.9	8.9	8.1	9.0
Children under 15 Present	0.8	0.8	0.4	0.5
TOTAL	100.0	100.1	100.0	100.0

SOURCE: U.S. Bureau of the Census, Census of Population and Housing (Washington, DC: U.S. Government Printing Office, 1960, 1970, and 1980); and Joint Center projections.

marriage necessarily means that two existing households combine to form one. Increases in the number of households due to separation and divorce, however, will help to offset these mergers. Over the next decade, the net effect of trends in marriage, divorce, and remarriage among the baby-boom generation will therefore be to stabilize the number of households they form.

In the last half of the decade, the shrinking cohorts of the end of the baby-boom and the baby-bust generations began to take over. Assuming that the baby-bust cohorts adopt the late-marriage patterns of their older siblings, the proportion married among cohorts in their twenties and early thirties will continue to decline during the next decade, and those who do marry will have fewer children.

Households

In order to derive the number of households from the projection of family nuclei, a household headship rate is applied to each group.[3] If cohort adjustments had remained the same in the past and could be expected to remain constant in the future, the choice of headship assumptions would be simple. As Chapter 3 pointed out, however, the housing transitions of birth cohorts varied considerably among the three analysis periods. In particular, headship rates for all cohorts rose 20 percent faster on average during 1970-1975 than during the 1960s or 1975-1980.

If household formation rates in the 1980s resemble those of the early 1970s, over 20 million new households will be added over the decade. Our analysis leads us to believe, however, that the high rates of the early 1970s are unusual and not likely to be repeated during this decade. Future cohort adjustments are more likely to resemble those occurring in the period 1975-1980, when growth in household headship slowed. Post-1980 data on household formation as well as increases in housing costs suggest that rates will continue to drop.

Indeed, a sluggish economy, together with an increase in the propensity of unmarried individuals to remain in their parental homes or to double up, could push the household formation rate down to 1.2 or 1.3 million per year. The most realistic projection, assuming a strong economy, is for household formation to continue at late 1970 rates, producing an increase of about 7.86 million households between 1980 and 1985 and 6.97 million between 1985 and 1990 (see Table 7.3). This implies that about 14.84 million

Table 7.3

HOUSEHOLD PROJECTIONS BY AGE OF HEAD
USING LATE 1970 HEADSHIP RATES, 1980-1990
(in thousands)

Age	1980 Households	1980-85		1985-90	
		Total	Annual Average	Total	Annual Average
< 25	8,580	-226	-45	-787	-157
25-29	9,979	1,104	221	193	39
30-34	9,493	1,256	251	1,284	257
35-44	13,928	3,436	687	3,338	668
45-54	12,447	-30	6	1,585	317
55-64	12,000	418	84	-607	-121
65-74	9,029	724	145	777	155
75+	5,633	1,182	236	1,190	238
TOTAL	81,089	7,864	1,573	6,974	1,395

Figures may not add up to totals due to rounding.

NOTE: Based on Annual Housing Survey estimates, which differ from census estimates. 1980 Census estimates broken down by age were not available at time of this writing. "Age" refers to age of female in married-couple households, and age of head in all other households.

SOURCE: U.S. Bureau of the Census, Census of Population and Households and Annual Housing Survey, 1980 (Washington, DC: U.S. Government Printing Office, 1980); and Joint Center projections.

more households would form over the decade at an annual
average rate of household formation of 1.48 million.

Homeownership

Using these population and family nucleus projections,
we can apply the cohort trend method to project homeownership rates. Different ownership rates for different population groups reflect life-cycle variations in housing
consumption patterns. As in the case of headship rates,
the 1975-1980 homeownership rate is preferable to earlier
rates.

Table 7.4 presents the Joint Center projections of
owner and renter households for 1985 and 1990. While the
aging of the population results in fewer households being
formed, it also increases the number of households that own
their residences. As Chapter 3 shows, the proportion of
homeowners is low among households headed by young adults
and tends to increase steadily with age. As the baby-boom
cohorts age, they will thus raise the number of owner
households without adding markedly to the total number of
households. We project that the number of households
owning their homes will grow by about 1.2 million. This
forecast implies that 68.0 percent of households will be
homeowners in 1990.

Housing Construction

In the 1970s, new construction added 20.9 million units
to the total housing inventory; with net losses estimated
at 2.6 million units, the nation's housing stock thus
increased 18.3 million units. Although there has been much
disagreement over the components of inventory change, it is
clear that net losses in the 1970s were substantially lower
than in the previous decade (i.e., 3.7 percent compared
with 10.9 percent in the 1960s). This decline in net
losses substantially reduced the amount of new construction
required to accommodate household growth and maintain the
level of vacant units.[4]

The dramatic reduction in net losses resulted from both
a decline in gross losses and an increase in non-new construction additions. Gross losses from the conventional
inventory (total units less mobile homes and seasonal
vacancies) fell from an estimated 10.7 percent over the
1960s to 7.6 percent during the 1970s. High losses among
mobile home units, however, offset some of this reduction

Table 7.4

HOUSEHOLDS BY TENURE, 1970-1990
(in thousands)

Tenure	Census 1970 (%)	Census 1980* (%)	Projected 1985 (%)	Projected 1990 (%)
Owners	40,504 (62.9%)	52,945 (65.3%)	54,121 (66.5%)	65,212 (68.0%)
Renters	23,924 (37.1%)	28,144 (34.8%)	29,831 (33.5%)	30,714 (32.0%)
TOTAL	64,428	81,089	88,952	95,927

Average Annual Change

	1970-1980	1980-1985	1985-1990
Owners	1,244	1,573	1,395
Renters	422	338	177
TOTAL	1,666	1,573	1,395

Figures may not add up to totals due to rounding.

*Derived from 1980 census population data and 1980 Annual Housing Survey.

SOURCE: U.W. Bureau of the Census, Census of Population and Households, 1970-1980, various tables (Washington, DC: U.S. Government Printing Office); and Joint Center projections.

in conventional losses: By the 1970s, mobile home losses were 19.0 percent of the total, up substantially from the 6.3 percent recorded in the 1960s. The rise in the proportion of mobile home losses reflects both the growth of these units as a percentage of the total inventory and the fact that mobile homes tend to have shorter useful lives than conventional housing.

The increase in non-new construction additions to the inventory also reduced net losses in the 1970s. Conversion of single-family homes into two or more units, adaptive re-use of commercial and industrial structures as residences, and other changes to the existing inventory added at least 2.7 million, and more likely as many as 3.9 million, units to the stock. It should be noted that even the lower of these two estimates is still nearly twice the number of non-new construction additions that the Bureau of the Census reported for the period 1960-1970.

Table 7.5 compares a baseline forecast for the 1980s consistent with these trends and the levels experienced in the 1970s. The baseline forecast estimates that 14.8 million households will form over the 1980s, a substantial decline from the 16.8 million in the previous decade. Assuming that the occupancy rate holds constant at the 1980 level of approximately 91 percent, the slowdown in household growth will produce a pronounced drop in the growth of housing units. If losses continue at rates observed during 1975-1980 and non-new construction provides the same share of total additions, gross losses for the decade would be 6.1 million units, non-new construction additions 3.4 million units, and net losses 2.6 million units. Lower household formation and fewer inventory losses imply that new construction will equal about 18.9 million units over the decade, including about 2.9 million mobile home placements.

Changing economic conditions could, of course, modify both household formation rates and net loss rates. If the sluggish economy and low levels of household formation experienced in the early 1980s continue, the estimate of 14.8 million new households could be too high; alternatively, a period of vigorous and sustained economic growth could push household growth to 15.8 million. Moreover, strong economic growth, together with the continued shift of households from city to suburb and from frostbelt to sunbelt, could raise loss rates in the 1980s. While it is unlikely that they will ever return to 1960 levels, net losses could increase to a decade rate of 4.0 percent.

Table 7.5

CHANGES IN TOTAL HOUSING STOCK, 1970–1990

Type of Stock	1970s (actual)		1980s (projected)	
	Millions of Units	Percentage of Initial Stock	Millions of Units	Percentage of Initial Stock
Beginning of Decade Stock	70.18	100.0	88.56	100.0
Growth of Total Stock	18.38	26.2	16.27	18.4
New Households	16.80	23.9	14.84	16.8
Additional Vacancies	1.59	2.3	1.43	1.6
New Construction plus				
Mobile Home Shipments	20.94	29.8	18.90	21.3
Net Loss	2.56	3.7	2.63	3.0
Gross Loss	6.50	9.3	6.07	6.9
Non-new Construction				
Additions	3.94	5.6	3.44	3.9
End of Decade Stock	88.56	126.2	104.83	118.4

NOTE: New households plus additional vacancies equals growth of total housing stock. Total growth also equals new construction plus mobile home shipments less net losses. Net losses equals gross losses less non-new construction additions.

SOURCE: U.S. Bureau of the Census, Census of Population and Housing, 1970 and 1980; Annual Housing Survey, 1973–1980 (Washington, DC: U.S. Government Printing Office); and Joint Center projections.

Table 7.6 shows how forecasts of new construction plus mobile home placements are affected by high and low estimates of household formation and net loss rates. Only a high rate of household formation together with a return to high net losses would induce new construction that would equal or exceed that of the 1970s. On the other hand, housing production could fall significantly given a low household growth rate. The most likely estimate, however, is 18.9 million units, or 10 percent lower than in the previous decade.

Despite this guarded assessment of housing production for the 1980s as a whole, it is important to note that new construction will increase sharply from the depressed levels experienced between 1980 and 1982; sustaining higher production into the late 1980s and 1990s, however, will be difficult. As the baby-boom generation ages, household formation rates and housing construction activity will begin a downward drift that will last until the year 2000. Moreover, not all the regions of the country will share equally in the new construction that does occur.

Table 7.6

FORECASTS OF NEW CONSTRUCTION PLUS MOBILE HOME
PLACEMENTS FOR THE 1980S UNDER THREE ASSUMPTIONS
OF HOUSEHOLD FORMATION AND NET LOSSES

Household Formation	Net Loss Rate		
	Low 2.0 Percent	Most Likely 3.0 Percent	High 4.0 Percent
Low 13.8 million	16.9	17.8	18.7
Most Likely 14.8 million	18.0	18.9	19.8
High 15.8 million	19.1	20.0	20.9

Figures are in millions of units.

SOURCE: Joint Center forecasts, June 1983. Most likely forecast for new construction plus mobile home placements is 18.9 million. Other forecasts are for discussion purposes only.

Regional Projections

Population

The regional variation in population and household growth observed in the 1970s is expected to continue in the 1980s. As Table 7.7 shows, the population of the Northeast grew by only 94,000 in the 1970s, with the New England states gaining 506,000 people and the Middle Atlantic states losing 412,000.

While the large central cities of the Northeast have been declining in population since the 1950s, by the 1970s numerous inner suburban areas were also losing residents. Joint Center projections suggest that population in the Middle Atlantic states will decrease by as much as 6.4 percent in the 1980s. Almost no population growth is forecast for the East North Central states. Having grown by only 3.5 percent in the 1970s, the population of these states is likely to increase by only 1.2 percent in the 1980s.

The population in the sunbelt, by contrast, is projected to grow significantly faster than the national average. Relative to the 1970s, however, the rate of population growth will decrease slightly in the Pacific and Mountain states and more sharply in the South Atlantic states.

As shown in Figure 7.1, the increase in young adults aged 25-34 will continue in all regions through the 1980s. Many of these young adults will be entering the housing market for the first time and should, therefore, stimulate housing construction. After 1990, though, all regions will feel the effects of the declining numbers.

Households

Although population growth is a major determinant of household growth, the number of households can increase at a greater rate than the number of people if average headship rates increase (or if average household size continues to decline). As the data in Table 7.8 indicate, the rate of household growth in the 1970s exceeded the rate of population growth in each of the nine census divisions. Even in the Middle Atlantic region, which lost population in the 1970s, the number of households grew by 10.3 percent.

Until we have completed our analysis of the 1980 Census Public Use tapes, it is not feasible to use the cohort

Table 7.7

POPULATION GROWTH BY REGION, 1970-1990
(in thousands)

Region and Division	Population			Decade Growth (%)	
	Actual 1970	Actual 1980	Forecast 1990	Actual 1970-80	Forecast 1980-90
Northeast	49,041	49,135	47,704	0.2	-2.9
New England	11,842	12,348	13,142	4.2	6.4
Middle Atlantic	37,199	36,787	34,562	-1.1	-6.4
North Central	56,572	58,854	61,274	4.0	4.1
East North Central	40,253	41,670	42,151	3.5	1.2
West North Central	16,319	17,184	19,123	5.3	11.3
South	62,795	75,353	89,921	20.0	19.3
South Atlantic	30,671	36,943	41,785	20.5	13.1
East South Central	12,803	14,663	18,079	14.5	23.3
West South Central	19,321	23,747	30,057	22.9	26.6
West	34,805	43,165	52,949	23.9	22.7
Mountain	8,282	11,368	15,416	37.2	35.6
Pacific	26,523	31,797	37,533	19.8	18.0
TOTAL	203,212	226,505	251,848	11.4	11.2

NOTE: Regional figures may not add up to national totals due to rounding.

SOURCE: George Masnick and John Pitkin, The Changing Population of States and Regions (Cambridge, MA: Joint Center for Urban Studies, 1982).

Figure 7.1

CHANGE IN NUMBER OF ADULTS AGED 25-34
BY CENSUS DIVISION, 1970-2000

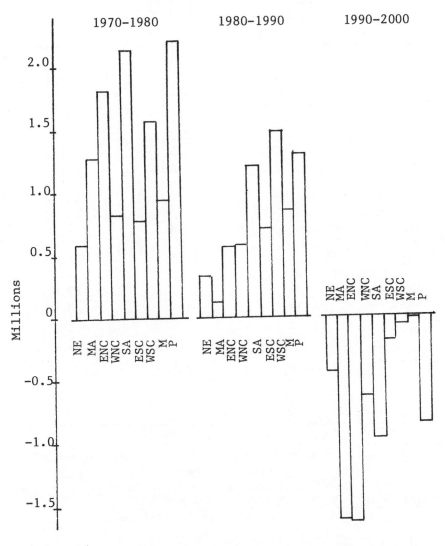

SOURCE: George Masnick and John Pitkin, The Changing
Population of State and Regions: Analysis and Projections
(Cambridge, MA: Joint Center for Urban Studies, 1982).

Table 7.8

COMPARISON OF POPULATION AND
HOUSEHOLD GROWTH RATES, 1970-1980

Region and Division	Population Growth Rate (%)	Household Growth Rate (%)
Northeast	0.2	12.4
New England	4.2	19.5
Middle Atlantic	-1.1	10.3
North Central	4.0	18.8
East North Central	3.5	18.2
West North Central	5.3	20.1
South	20.0	37.1
South Atlantic	20.5	39.0
East South Central	14.5	29.8
West South Central	22.9	39.0
West	23.9	39.2
Mountain	37.2	58.1
Pacific	19.8	33.7
TOTAL	11.4	26.4

SOURCES: Population rates from the U.S. Bureau of the
Census, Census of Population: General Characteristics, 1970
and 1980; household rates from Census Summary Tape Files,
First Count, 1970; and Summary Tape Files 1C, 1980 (Washington, DC: U.S. Government Printing Office).

approach to project regional growth in the number of house-holds. Over the 1970s, however, the regional variation in aggregate headship rates (total number of heads of house-holds divided by total population) was not very large, ranging from New England (about three percent lower than the U.S. average) to the Mountain and Pacific regions (between two and four percent higher). Even though much larger differences exist across regions in marital status and in headship rates specific to marital status and age categories, these variations disappear when all categories are combined. The reason for this uniformity is not clear.

Given the major changes that occurred in the 1970s in patterns and headship rates of single, divorced, and widowed men and women in each region, it is even more surprising that the regional variations in crude aggregate headship were relatively stable over time. As Table 7.9 indicates, in only three regions do the ratios of observed to expected household growth using national headship rates differ by more than one percent between 1970 and 1980. Headship rates were lower by about one percent in the Middle Atlantic region relative to the national average, and by about two percent in the Pacific region, but higher by about one percent in the Mountain states. Rates in all other regions remained parallel to the national trend. It appears that especially tight housing markets in the Middle Atlantic and Pacific regions served to drive headship rates down, while prosperity in the Mountain states attracted a large number of migrants who tended to live in independent households.

Since we do not fully understand why this stability existed over the past decade, it is difficult to predict with certainty that it will continue over the next. With this qualification in mind, Table 7.10 presents preliminary regional projections of total households, based on the Joint Center's regional population forecasts and the assumption that the crude aggregate headship rate will remain consistent across regions.

Households will continue to increase at a faster rate than the population, but the difference will be less pro-nounced. While the projected total population increase of 25 million is larger than that experienced in the 1970s, household growth is projected to drop from 17.5 to 14.8 million. Even sharper declines are expected for selected regions: In the Middle Atlantic states, for example, household growth is forecast to fall from 1.3 to 0.1

Table 7.9

RATIO OF ACTUAL REGIONAL HOUSEHOLDS TO HYPOTHETICAL
HOUSEHOLDS DERIVED FROM NATIONAL HEADSHIP RATES, 1970-1980

Division	1970	1980	Change 1970-1980
Northeast			
New England	.9719	.9686	-.0033
Middle Atlantic	.9808	.9701	-.0107
North Central			
East North Central	.9987	1.0039	.0052
West North Central	1.0196	1.0191	-.0005
South			
South Atlantic	.9892	.9902	.0010
East South Central	.9862	.9926	.0064
West South Central	1.0126	1.0207	.0081
West			.
Mountain	1.0232	1.0334	.0102
Pacific	1.0402	1.0197	-.0205
TOTAL	1.0000	1.0000	1.0000

SOURCES: Population rates from U.S. Bureau of the Census,
Census of Population: General Characteristics, 1970 and
1980; household rates from Census Summary Tape Files, First
Count, 1970, and Summary Tape Files 1C, 1980 (Washington,
DC: U.S. Government Printing Office).

Table 7.10

OBSERVED AND PROJECTED CHANGE IN HOUSEHOLDS BY REGION, 1960-1990
(in millions)

Census Division	Total Number of Households				Increase over Decade		
	1960	1970	1980	1990	1960-70	1970-80	1980-90
Northeast	3.12	3.65	4.39	5.06	0.53	0.74	0.67
Middle Atlantic	10.14	11.88	13.21	13.32	1.74	1.33	0.11
East North Central	10.71	12.41	14.79	15.97	1.70	2.38	1.18
West North Central	4.67	5.17	6.26	7.35	0.50	1.09	1.09
South Atlantic	7.27	9.47	13.27	16.15	2.20	3.80	2.88
East South Central	3.31	3.89	5.09	6.66	0.58	1.20	1.57
West South Central	4.93	5.97	8.37	11.17	1.04	2.40	2.80
Mountain	1.98	2.53	4.04	5.77	0.55	1.51	1.73
Pacific	6.65	8.67	11.68	14.49	2.02	3.01	2.81
TOTAL	53.02	63.64	81.09	95.93	10.62	17.45	14.84

NOTE: Regional figures may not add up to national totals due to rounding.

SOURCE: 1960 and 1970 numbers from decennial census. 1980 numbers from applying Annual Housing Survey headship rates to 1980 census population data.

million. The largest growth (of about 2.8 million households) is projected to occur in the South Atlantic, West
South Central, and Pacific divisions. Three regions (East
South Central, West South Central, and Mountain) are expected to experience more household growth in the 1980s
than in the 1970s.

The regional distribution of household growth appears
in Table 7.11. The projected near-zero net growth in the
Middle Atlantic division deserves comment. Three factors
combine to reduce the number of households: out-migration;
delayed family formation among the remaining young adults;
and lower-than-average headship rates among the unmarried
population. Our population projections assume a net loss
of about 7 million persons from the cohort that was aged
15-24 in 1980. Such a level of out-migration is consistent
with optimism about national economic growth: with greater

Table 7.11

HOUSEHOLD GROWTH BY REGION, 1960-1990

Region and Division	1960-1970	1970-1980	1960-1980
Northeast			
New England	5.0	4.2	4.5
Middle Atlantic	13.9	7.3	0.7
North Central			
East North Central	16.0	13.5	8.0
West North Central	4.7	6.2	7.3
South			
South Atlantic	20.7	22.0	19.4
East South Central	5.5	6.9	10.6
West South Central	9.8	13.9	18.9
West			
Mountain	5.2	8.8	11.7
Pacific	19.0	17.4	18.9
TOTAL	100.0	100.0	100.0

All figures are percentage changes.

SOURCE: U.S. Bureau of the Census, Census of Population and Households, 1960-1980, various tables; and Joint
Center projections.

prosperity, more migrants would likely seek the greater employment opportunities of the South and West. On the other hand, a lackluster economy could cause mobility rates to fall as young adults remain in their parental households because of job insecurity and the high cost of housing. Although economic recession may thus keep more of the baby-boom generation in the Middle Atlantic states, it would also tend to depress headship rates. On balance, then, different economic assumptions would probably have only a modest impact on household forecasts.

In the final analysis, it may be that the simplified assumptions used to project regional shares of total household growth are not valid for the Middle Atlantic states. For example, high levels of out-migration might release pressure on the housing market enough to allow higher rates of household formation. Alternatively, lower rates of out-migration might increase the demand for new housing, which, if supplied, could likewise lead to stable rather than declining headship rates. When the appropriate analysis of 1980 census data is completed, the calculation of cohort headship trends for separate types of family nuclei in each region will help resolve this ambiguity.

Housing Construction

Regional trends in new construction, conversions, and losses depend on the distribution of population and economic activity across and within individual regions. Over time, shifts in the spatial distribution of population and employment increase housing demand in some areas at the expense of others. Even within a given area, changes in incomes or in the composition of population may change the number of households of a particular type and thus the housing that they demand.

The Joint Center forecasts a slowdown in growth of households and in housing demand nationwide. Combined with more intensive use of the existing inventory, this means that housing starts will also fall. Further declines in new housing production are likely in the 1990s as the decreasing population of the baby-bust generation moves into the family-formation ages.

As household growth slows, forecasts of total construction activity are increasingly influenced by the other components of inventory change (i.e., vacancies, losses, and non-new construction additions). As shown in Table 7.12, in the Middle Atlantic region, for example, households will

Table 7.12

COMPONENTS OF INVENTORY CHANGE BY REGION, 1980-1990
(thousands of units)

Region	Households	Additional Vacancies	Losses	Total Additions	Non-new Construction Additions	New Construction Plus Mobile Home Placements
Northeast	780	80	1,333	2,139	596	1,597
New England	670	70	338	1,078	293	785
Middle Atlantic	110	10	995	1,115	303	812
North Central	2,270	20	1,654	4,124	500	3,624
East North Central	1,180	10	1,146	2,426	294	2,132
West North Central	1,090	10	508	1,698	206	1,492
South	7,250	720	2,339	10,309	1,622	8,687
South Atlantic	2,880	300	1,180	4,360	686	3,674
East South Central	1,570	120	450	2,140	337	1,803
West South Central	2,800	300	709	3,809	599	3,210
West	4,540	430	742	5,712	723	4,989
Mountain	1,730	210	204	2,144	271	1,873
Pacific	2,810	220	538	3,568	452	3,116
TOTAL	14,840	1,430	6,068	22,338	3,441	18,897

SOURCE: Joint Center projections.

increase by only 110,000 in the 1980s, but new construction for the decade will equal 812,000 units. This difference is largely due to the new housing needed to offset the nearly one million units that will be lost during the decade. In forming these estimates, it was assumed that the vacancy rate would remain unchanged, an assumption consistent with historical experience. As household growth slows to near zero in this division, however, it is possible that vacancies will increase. If the vacancy rate for the Middle Atlantic states were to rise by one percent, the housing stock (and hence new construction) would have to increase by an additional 140,000 units. The distributions in Table 7.12 also demonstrate the importance of non-new construction additions as a source of housing supply. In the Northeast, such additions will account for approximately 25 percent of total additions.

New construction levels and the use of the existing inventory in a given area also depend on inter- and intra-regional population flows, as regional housing market activity becomes in effect a zero-sum game. If households continue to flee from some inner-city neighborhoods and flock to others, and to move from large metropolitan areas to small towns and rural areas, high losses in some areas will be offset by intensive use of the inventory in other areas. Although less well documented than broad population shifts from one region to the next, intra-regional movements of people and jobs are important in understanding emerging patterns of housing market activity.

The continued movement of jobs and population from frostbelt to sunbelt, and from central city to suburb and non-metropolitan areas, also has important implications for housing losses and non-new construction additions. In the fast-growth regions of the South and West, as well as in the non-metropolitan portions of the Northeast and North Central regions, growth in the number of households will be an incentive for property owners to maintain and rehabilitate their structures. As a result, inventory losses in these areas are likely to remain at or below the low levels reported in the 1970s. For the central cities of the Northeast and North Central regions, however, the prospect is bleak; the slow and frequently negative change in the total number of households ensures continuing high levels of inventory losses, a problem that plagued many large central cities in the 1970s.

While continuing high losses in the Northeast and North Central areas will create some demand for new construction

and non-new construction additions, the flow of population
and households away from certain frostbelt states suggests
that these regions will capture smaller shares of national
new housing market activity in the 1980s. As Table 7.13
indicates, the biggest declines in the shares of total
housing production will occur in the Middle Atlantic and
East North Central states, while both New England and the
West North Central divisions will experience slight increases. The Northeast and North Central regions combined
will capture only 27.7 percent of new construction and
mobile home placements in the 1980s, down from 33.9 percent
in the 1970s.

Table 7.13

HOUSEHOLD GROWTH AND NEW CONSTRUCTION PLUS
MOBILE HOME SHIPMENTS, BY REGION, 1970-1990
(as percentages of total

Region and Division	Household Growth (%)		New Construction Plus Mobile Home Shipments (%)	
	1970-80	1980-90	1970-80	1980-90
Northeast	11.5	5.3	11.8	8.5
New England	4.2	4.5	3.6	4.2
Middle Atlantic	7.3	0.7	8.3	4.3
North Central	19.7	15.3	22.1	19.2
East North Central	13.5	8.0	14.7	11.3
West North Central	6.2	7.3	7.4	7.9
South	42.8	48.9	42.4	45.9
South Atlantic	22.0	19.4	21.5	19.4
East South Central	6.9	10.6	7.5	9.5
West South Central	13.9	18.9	13.4	17.0
West	26.1	30.6	23.7	26.4
Mountain	8.7	11.7	8.1	9.9
Pacific	17.4	18.9	15.6	16.5
TOTAL	100.0	100.0	100.0	100.0

SOURCE: U.S. Bureau of the Census, 1980 Census of
Population, Standard Metropolitan Statistical Areas - 1980,
supplementary reports PC80-S1-5; and Joint Center projections, June 1983.

NOTES

1. See George S. Masnick and John Pitkin, The Changing Populations of States and Regions: Analysis and Projections, 1970-2000 (Cambridge, MA: Joint Center for Urban Studies, 1982); and U.S. Bureau of the Census, Advance Report, Current Population Report, series P-25, no. 922 (Washington, D.C.: U.S. Government Printing Office, 1980).

2. John Pitkin and George Masnick, "Projections of Housing Consumption in the U.S., 1980 to 2000, by a Cohort Method," Annual Housing Survey Studies, no. 9 (June 1980). For the nation as a whole, we have analyzed cohort behavior with respect to population growth, marital status, family size, headship, and housing consumption by following the aging of 16 family nuclei categories defined by sex, marital status, and family size over the period since World War II.

3. These new projections differ from earlier Joint Center forecasts in two ways. First, the series using the headship trends of the 1960-1970 period (series 2-B[R]) have been dropped and replaced by the series from the 1975-1980 period. Second, the starting point for the new projections is the 1980 census population data, transformed into households using 1980 Annual Housing Survey headship rates. The earlier Joint Center forecasts are found in John Pitkin and George Masnick, "Linking Projections of Households with Housing Consumption: An Exploration of Alternative Series" (report prepared for the Office of Policy Development and Research, Department of Housing and Urban Development, 1981).

4. For a more detailed discussion of the components of inventory change, see William C. Apgar, Jr., "The Changing Utilization of the Housing Inventory: Past Trends and Future Prospects," Working Paper no. W83-1 (Cambridge, MA: Joint Center for Urban Studies, revised July 1983).

8

INTERPRETING THE OUTLOOK

This book has examined the basic factors that are likely to influence the housing market over the next 10 to 20 years. This of course is a difficult undertaking since the housing industry is responsive to both powerful long-term trends in the composition and regional distribution of the population and short-term fluctuations in mortgage interest rates and other economic variables. Distinguishing the short-term effects of business cycles from longer-term trends is the essence of long-range forecasting.

Unfortunately, many long-term forecasts are little more than extrapolations of recent events. Based on the strong performance of the housing industry in the late 1970s, many analysts asserted that the 1980s would be a period of vigorous growth. Numerous forecasters predicted that the decade would witness record levels of household formation, housing starts, and mobile home placements. The deep recession of 1980 to 1982, however, led many forecasters to alter radically their assessments of the 1980s. Serious discussion centered on the consequences of having as few as 10 million conventional housing starts for the entire decade, a figure that would represent a 30 to 50 percent decline from the record production levels of the 1970s.

In contrast to the volatility of the predictions prepared by many forecasting organizations, the Joint Center estimates presented since the publication of the previous Housing Outlook Reports have been quite stable. First published in 1979, Joint Center forecasts of household

formation for the 1980s were criticized as being too pessimistic. While these predictions have been somewhat revised
to reflect new data obtained from the 1980 Census of Population, they are substantially the same as those presented
in this book. In the interim, however, many other analysts
reduced their estimates of household formation and housing
market activity. As a result, the Joint Center forecasts
may in fact appear to be somewhat less pessimistic than
many other current predictions for the 1980s.

The consistency of the Joint Center forecasts over the
last several years reflects the fact they are based on an
assessment of likely trends in both the national economy
and the composition and place of residence of population
and households. While forecasts of long-term trends in
many economic variables have changed dramatically over the
past five years, basic demographic and mobility patterns
have been relatively stable. Compared to estimates of
likely federal budget deficits, mortgage rates, or other
economic variables, demographic predictions over the period
have proven to be quite reliable.

Variation in mortgage interest rates and other economic
variables has more impact on housing market activity in the
short run than in the long run. Since real estate is a
long-lived capital asset, property owners and homeowners
tend to delay such purchases during periods of high mortgage interest rates. But as the high levels of housing
sales in 1983 suggest, once households and investors
believe that interest rates have reached a cyclical low,
many are willing to enter the housing market, even if in
absolute terms mortgage interest rates remain high. Similarly, high rates of unemployment in 1981 and 1982 reduced
consumer confidence and dampened willingness to assume new
long-term debts. Yet with the upturn in the economy and
the reduction of unemployment in 1983, households again
were eager to borrow funds to finance housing purchases.

Unlike interest rates, short-term changes in demographic factors, mobility patterns, and changes in home-
building technology have little effect on housing activity.
The 60 percent jump in housing starts in 1983 had little to
do with short-term changes in trends in the composition of
the population, their place of residence, or the production
technology available to the home building sector. These
factors, however, take on greater weight over a longer
term. Thus the movement of population from frostbelt to
sunbelt and the changing characteristics of households will
affect the number, characteristics, and price of homes

built.   The influence of these longer-term trends on the
housing industry transcends business cycles, though often
their presence is obscured by cyclical variation.

Many forecasts fall short in presenting useful views of
the future of housing industry activity by failing ade-
quately to distinguish cycles from trends.   While it is
appropriate to adjust forecasts to reflect changing assessments of factors that influence the housing industry over
time, the fact that the first three years of the 1980s
spanned the worst recession since World War II should make
us particularly wary in extrapolating from recent events
and weighing their implications.

If the future is not a simple extension of recent
changes, neither will the 1980s simply mirror the longer-
term trends of the 1960s and 1970s.   Relative to past
decades, housing industry activity will be somewhat sub-
dued, with household formation and housing starts falling
some 15 percent below 1970 levels.   As a result of the
changing structure of the nation's housing finance system,
homeowners and other owners of residential real estate must
compete in the national capital markets for financial
resources.   Moreover, there can be little doubt that continuation of large federal budget deficits and investor
uncertainty concerning long-term inflation rates will keep
mortgage interest rates at relatively high levels for the
remainder of the decade.

While conceding that affordability will continue to
constrain housing market activity, particularly the housing
choices of moderate- and low-income families and households, we have argued throughout this book that affordability is only one of the factors that will influence the
housing industry in the 1980s.   The extent to which affordability problems dampen housing market activity depends, of
course, on the strength of the desire of households to
upgrade their housing and the availability of the financial
resources required.   In a period of persistently high real
interest rates, the plans of many households will undoubtedly be scaled down.   Over the longer term, however,
some of the adverse effects of higher mortgage rates will
be offset by increases in real incomes.   Increasing labor
force participation combined with higher per capita income
through productivity improvements will lead to higher
household real income throughout the remainder of the
1980s.

Finally, the aging of the baby-boom generation and continuing growth of lower-density and hence lower-cost areas

of the country will serve to enhance housing consumption in the 1980s. In certain areas of the country, the changing utilization of the existing inventory, particularly the sustained high level of conversion of single-family homes into multiple units and nonresidential structures into housing and the reduced levels of inventory losses, will somewhat reduce new construction requirements. In these areas, the opportunities for investment in the existing inventory will offset declines in new construction.

Although it is easy to assume that one factor will dominate the future, in fact housing market activity results from a complex interaction of demographics, housing choices, housing finance, government policy, and housing technology. In light of this complexity, it is important to recognize that there are many aspects of housing market behavior that are crucial for forecasting that no responsible person would claim to comprehend fully. In attempting to place recent events into a longer-term historical perspective, this book has attempted to provide a firm foundation for assessing likely future trends in the housing industry and a road map for guiding future housing market research.

Interpreting Recent Events

For much of the postwar period, the housing situation of most U.S. households improved substantially. Echoing the conclusion of many policy analysts, the recently released report of the President's Commission on Housing declared that "basic data point to a continuing improvement in the housing of most Americans."[1] Particularly impressive were the declines in the real cost of housing. As noted earlier, throughout much of the postwar period the cost of rental housing, adjusted for inflation, declined. Moreover, although interest rates and the purchase price of dwelling units moved up steadily in the 1960s and 1970s, the total cost of owning a home, adjusted for the expected capital gains and tax advantages of homeownership, declined steadily for much of the period and may even have turned negative between 1977 and 1979.

With the downturn in the general economy in 1980, the cost of owning a home increased sharply. By 1982, higher home prices, interest rates, and utility costs--together with a reduction in the expected capital gains from appreciation--combined to raise the total costs of owning a home to nearly 40 percent of the median family income, the highest in more than 30 years.

The increase in the costs of homeownership has been matched in recent years by equally significant increases in the cost of rental housing. Throughout much of the 1960s and 1970s, increases in rents lagged behind increases in other consumer prices, even though the widely cited consumer price rent index substantially overstated the extent of this lag. Since 1981, however, real rents have turned up sharply in many areas. Nationwide, from 1981 to 1983, real rents may have increased by as much as eight percent.

The rapid increases in the cost of owner- and renter-occupied housing had a dramatic effect on the nation's housing market. During the period 1980 to 1983, the annual average increase in household formation fell to less than 1 million, after averaging 1.7 million annually during the 1970s. Indeed, for the single year from March 1982 to March 1983, the increase in the number of households was only 391,000. Faced with rising real rents and high levels of unemployment, many young persons remained at home with their parents, shared apartments with friends or relatives, or remained in college dormitories. The result was a marked slowdown in the rate of growth of young single-person households.

Mobility also declined. American households have traditionally expected to improve their housing conditions by periodically moving to a better unit. With the exceptions of the 1975 recession and the boom years of 1977-1978, mobility rates (that is, the percentage of households changing place of residence over a one-year period) remained relatively constant until 1979. By 1981, however, mobility rates had fallen to 17.6 percent, from an average of 19.5 percent in the previous eight years. If mobility had remained at normal levels, an additional 1.6 million households would have changed residence in that year.

The slowdown in household formation and mobility generated an equally pronouced slowdown in sales of existing and new single-family houses. Moreover, those households that did move were less likely to purchase a home than in previous years. Only 58.4 percent of homeowners who moved in 1980 bought their next unit, down from over 70 percent in the previous year. The likelihood that a young, low-income renter household would buy dropped from 14.6 to only 7.9 percent. As a result of these changes in homebuying activity, for the first time in perhaps 50 years, the share of households owning their own home declined, from 65.8 percent in 1980 to 64.8 percent in 1983.

In addition to lower mobility and homeownership rates, higher housing costs generated a change in the types of homes that consumers purchased. While multi-family housing boomed in the late 1960s and early 1970s, single-family construction activity rebounded, and from 1975 to 1977 accounted for about three-quarters of all private housing starts. By 1982, however, the single-family share had fallen to 62.7 percent. With condominiums, townhouses, and other higher-density types of housing gaining in proportion, many analysts noted that higher housing costs were shifting homebuyers away from traditional single-family units. Moreover, from 1979 to 1982, the average size of new single-family homes (both attached and detached) also declined, a trend that was widely interpreted as a sign that increased housing costs were constraining the size of homes that households were able to purchase.

In light of the relatively sharp increases in the cost of housing since 1979, perhaps the most surprising aspect of the most recent housing recession was not that home-ownership declined, or that the size of new homes de-creased, but rather by how little they fell. The rate of homeownership declined, but the absolute number of home-owners increased. Thus, by the end of what many analysts considered to be the most severe recession in 50 years, there were more homeowners than at any other time in the nation's history. The average size of new single-family homes (attached and detached) did decline by 2.8 percent from 1,760 square feet in 1979 to 1,710 in 1982, but this decline was neither unique nor particularly severe by historical standards. In each of the previous two periods of declining housing construction activity, namely 1969 to 1970, and 1974 to 1975, the average size of new single-family homes decreased as well. From 1969 to 1970, the size of new single-family homes declined by 6.5 percent, and from 1974 to 1975 by 3.0 percent.

Just as the decline in single-family home sizes during the period 1979 to 1982 was not unprecedented, neither was the upturn in 1983. Following the housing recessions of 1969-1970 and 1974-1975, the size of completed new single-family homes increased with quickening new construction activity. This pattern held in 1983. Although the number of small single-family homes completed in 1983 also rose, the sharpest increases were recorded in the larger homes. From 1982 to 1983, the number of new homes completed with

less than 1,000 square feet increased by only 24.6 percent,
and the number with 1,000 to 1,200 square feet increased by
only 25.0 percent. By contrast, homes with more than 2,400
square feet were up by 44.2 percent, while even sharper
increases were recorded for homes with 1,600 to 2,000
square feet (61.9 percent), and with 2,000 to 2,400 square
feet (54.3 percent).

In interpreting the decline in the size of homes that
occurred from 1979 to 1982 as the beginning of a new long-
term trend, analysts ignored important cyclical aspects of
the housing industry. Not only did the new construction
market turn down sharply in the late 1970s, so did the
housing resale market. Increasing from the 1974 low of
2.2 million, existing single-family home sales moved up
steadily to the 1978 record figure of 3.98 million. Sales
in 1979 were nearly as good, totaling 3.83 million, but
fell off sharply to 2.42 million in 1981, and to slightly
under 2 million in 1982.

The slump in sales activity in the period 1979 to 1982
changed the composition of potential homebuyers. Annual
Housing Survey statistics indicate that, in 1978, 3.0
million previous owners purchased a dwelling unit. This
fell to 2.0 million in 1981, the most recent year Annual
Housing Survey data are available. The 33 percent decline
in the number of previous owners purchasing homes is, of
course, simply the mirror image of the decrease in home
sales that occurred during the period. It is significant
that Annual Housing Survey data indicate that the number of
first-time buyers fell off by only 20 percent, declining
from 2.0 million in 1978 to 1.6 million in 1981.

The fact that the number of first-time buyers may be
less cyclically sensitive than the number of all buyers may
seem counterintuitive, since first-time buyers tend to be
younger, and have less income and wealth than other buyers.
Yet it is important to note that the first-time buyer also
does not have the problem of first selling an existing
home. For the trade-up buyers, high interest rates reduce
the likely sale price of their existing home and increase
the carrying costs associated with their new home. Since
the potential trade-up buyer already owns a house, he or
she can delay purchase and continue to enjoy the tax and
other benefits associated with owning a home. Delay for
the first-time buyer, however, involves loss of the tax
benefit and other advantages of ownership. Thus, during
the recent decline in sales and starts activity, a surprisingly large number of first-time buyers stayed in the

market, while a greater proportion of the trade-up buyers
dropped out. This in turn shifted the demand away from
larger detached homes, and helps explain the change in the
mix of construction activity that occurred during the
period.

As these comments suggest, an active resale market
benefits the new construction industry. Households able to
sell an existing home bring to the marketplace the capital
gains made from the sale of their previous unit. As
interest rates turned down in late 1982, sales of existing
and new homes turned up. In 1983, 2.7 million homes were
sold, an impressive 36.5 percent increase over the previous
year. While first-time buyers increased, the combination
of lower housing costs and the increase in the number of
trade-up buyers undoubtedly were central factors behind the
strong growth in demand for larger single-family detached
homes.

Since both the level and the mix of new construction
appear to be cyclically sensitive, a return to high
interest rates and a decline in the sales of existing
homes could result in a decline in the demand for larger
single-family detached homes. In the long run, however,
demographic factors, mobility patterns, and the changing
utilization of the existing inventory should combine to
generate a relatively healthy environment for the construction of larger detached homes. Thus, despite the expected
slowdown in total housing construction activity, the 1980s
will nevertheless be a period of increased rates of homeownership, growth of single-family detached housing, and
continued production of larger homes.

The Aging of the Baby Boom

If the 1970s were the decade of the young single-person
household, then the 1980s will see a growth of middle-aged
families and individuals. With today's emphasis on health,
the term middle-aged may be somewhat elusive, but the
simple fact is that the leading edge of the baby-boom
generation, those born between 1946 and 1955, will be from
35 to 45 years old by 1990. As a result, the age group 35
to 45 is the fastest-growing segment of the U.S. population. In the 1970s, the number of 35- to 45-year-olds
increased by 11 percent. In the 1980s, this group will
grow by 47 percent.

In sharp contrast, the growth in the number of young
adults is slowing markedly. In the 1970s, the population

aged 20 to 35 increased by 41.4 percent. In the 1980s, this age group will increase by only 7.8 percent, and in the 1990s the number of young adults will actually begin to decline.

As a result of the aging of the baby-boom generation, household growth is not evenly distributed by age of household head. As discussed in Chapter 7, the number of households is projected to increase by 14.8 million, or 18.3 percent during the 1980s. Households with heads aged 35 to 45 will increase 48.6 percent in the 1980s, while households with heads aged 20 to 35 will grow by only 10.1 percent. Thus increases in households with heads aged 35 to 45 account for 6.8 million of the predicted increase of 14.8 million in the total number of households in the 1980s. Households aged 25 to 35 will grow by only 3.8 million, while households with a head less than 25 years of age will actually decline by nearly 1 million from 1980 to 1990.

The aging of the baby boom has important implications for the mix of new construction. Not all baby-boomers will marry, but most will. Not all women born between 1945 and 1955 will bear children, but Joint Center forecasts suggest that 80 percent of all women will have at least one child, and 45 percent will have two or more children. While the 1970s were oriented toward younger, single-person households, the 1980s will be more oriented toward a somewhat older, more family-type household. At the same time, these baby-boom families are just now reaching their highest earnings potential. Both demographic and income factors related to the aging of the baby boom should generate continued demand for larger, single-family detached homes for the rest of the 1980s and into the 1990s.

Changing Utilization of the Existing Inventory

As noted earlier, conversion, rehabilitation, alteration, repairs, and additions to the existing inventory are likely to capture a larger share of total residential investment in the 1980s. In the 1970s, conversion of single-family homes into two or more units added more than 800,000 units to the inventory. The conversion of non-residential buildings into residential units may have added another 800,000 units, while restoration of vacant units, conversion of hotels, dormitories, and other residential properties into year-round housing units may have added another 800,000 units. In all, non-new construction activity added 2.6 million units to the inventory in the 1970s.

Equally important in adding to the inventory was the increased extent to which households were investing in maintaining existing structures. In part this reflects the increasing costs of purchasing a new or existing home. As housing costs increased, many households purchased and repaired older housing units. In addition, the increased maintenance efforts reflected the fact that the housing inventory was increasingly worthy of preservation. By 1980, three out of every five dwelling units had been built since 1950, with the vast majority of this inventory located in communities with modern land use and building codes. Unlike much of the substandard housing that was built in unregulated rural areas or crowded urban areas, much of this newer housing was solidly constructed and located in residential communities with adequate basic public services. As housing costs increased, the value of these well-built structures increased accordingly, adding to the incentive of property owners to protect their investment with an adequate maintenance plan.

As a result of the improved quality of the structures and the greater emphasis on maintenance, inventory losses fell sharply in the 1970s. Losses are projected in the 1980s to average 500,000 to 600,000 per year, down sharply from the loss figures of the 1950s and 1960s. Since in the 1950s and 1960s losses were concentrated in the multi-family portion of the inventory, the reduction in the absolute number of losses is most pronounced for multi-family units. In addition, as the mobile home portion of the inventory increases, mobile home losses are likely to account for increasing shares of the housing losses in the 1980s.

The combination of lower household formation, more non-new construction additions, and reduced losses points to reduced levels of housing construction for the decades ahead. Construction of conventional units should average 1.4 to 1.6 million units per year for the decade, while mobile home production could add another 250 to 300 thousand units per year. In addition to affecting total production levels, the changing utilization of the existing inventory also has implications for the types of new construction activity. Reduced loss rates and increased non-new construction activity, which typically adds multi-family units, reduce multi-family construction require-

ments. In short, even if housing costs and other factors
point to increased demand for multi-family units, this need
not result in increased multi-family new construction.
Alhough exact numbers are difficult to predict, at least a
portion of the future supply of multi-family units will be
provided through non-new construction.

Decentralization of Housing Industry Activity

Alhough housing analysts typically focus on the extent
to which changes in the national economy will alter mortgage interest rates, utility costs, or other factors important to the cost of housing of different types, the cost
of a new unit will also depend to an important degree on
its location. Labor costs, material costs, and especially
land costs vary from one region to the next, and within
regions from high-density, central-city areas to lower-
density, non-metropolitan areas.

The decentralization of housing industry activity has
important implications for the mix of new construction.
Decentralization includes not only the movement of people
and jobs from the frostbelt to the sunbelt, but also from
larger metropolitan areas to smaller metropolitan and
non-metropolitan areas. In the late 1970s, non-metropolitan
areas captured 42 percent of all the starts of single-
family homes. Some of this growth was simply the spillover
from metropolitan areas into adjacent counties.   But as
noted earlier, to a surprising extent, the 1970s witnessed
new growth in many previously slow-growth, isolated counties.   Moreover, much of this non-metropolitan growth
involved in-migration of family households.   During the
1970s single-person households continued to move, on net,
into metropolitan areas, while family households, particularly young families, were increasingly attracted to the
advantages of living in low-density, non-metropolitan
areas.

This trend, together with the increasing family households of the aging baby boom, has an important effect on
the types of new units built. Single-family homes comprise
by far the largest share of new construction activity in
low-density, non-metropolitan areas.   In the late 1970s,
single-family homes accounted for 90 percent of the housing
starts in non-metropolitan areas.   Continuation of growth
in lower-density areas is an important factor in our forecast that single-family detached homes will continue to

account for a large share of total conventional housing
starts in the remainder of the 1980s.

The Joint Center expectation of a continuing healthy
single-family market stands in contrast to the many predictions that this traditional form of housing is a relic of
past decades. Many analysts predict that the decline of
household size and the continuation of high housing costs
will stimulate greater production of less expensive townhouses or other forms of land-efficient types of construction. Such approaches can substantially lower housing
production costs in areas with high land costs. Yet it is
important to recognize that economizing on land costs
offers only small cost savings in many fast-growing, lower-
density communities. In these low land-cost areas, reducing housing costs must be linked to reductions in the cost
of the structure. As a result, it is interesting to note
that while higher costs were stimulating more land-
intensive development in higher-density areas, in lower-
density areas the mobile home was the primary beneficiary
of the inability of many first-time buyers to afford conventional single-family homes.

The emphasis on mobile homes should change as the
residents of these lower-density areas age. As noted
earlier, much of the projected increase in the number of
younger and middle-aged households will occur in the South
and the West, and in particular in many of the smaller
SMSAs and lower-density, non-metropolitan areas of these
regions. The growth of households due to the migration of
young families into these lower-density places should
further add to the demand for larger, single-family homes.
Historically, many of the fastest-growing areas in the
South and the West lagged behind the rest of the country
in terms of the size and quality of their housing inventory. In terms of size of units, the best housing is
located in the suburban portions of metropolitan areas of
the Northeast, where nearly one of every three units has
seven or more rooms. By contrast, only 17 percent of the
dwelling units in the non-metropolitan South, and 25
percent in the suburban South, have more than seven rooms.
In short, some of the fastest-growth areas of the country
are ill-equipped to house the increasing baby-boom
households. Even if affordability problems persist for the
rest of the decade, this mismatch of supply and demand will
spark continued construction of larger units in the fast-
growth areas.

Housing Policy in the 1980s

Since both the level and the mix of new construction appear to be affected by cyclical variations, a return to high interest rates or the start of a prolonged period of economic decline would make it likely that housing starts in the 1980s would fail to reach the predicted level or that the industry could witness a longer-term decline in the demand for larger single-family detached homes. This is simply a reminder that, as well as changes in basic demographic trends, changes in public policy could change the housing outlook. While presenting no explicit forecast of public policy, implicit in this outlook for housing is the assumption that housing policy will continue along the same general path established in the late 1970s and early 1980s. This includes, among other things, a reduced federal role in providing direct subsidies for low- and moderate-income households, and increased involvement of state and local governments in issues of housing and economic and community development. This last section points out some of the major issues confronting public decision makers as the nation moves forward into the 1980s.

Providing Assistance for the Housing Have-nots. T h e period of sustained inflation not only distorted national financial markets, but also served to widen the gap between the housing haves and the housing have-nots. Homeowners who accrued substantial capital gains in the 1970s are still enjoying the benefits: Those who choose to move can use this accumulated equity to help defray the cost of purchasing another home. Those who remain in their current homes benefit as well. Borrowing against accumulated home equity, once an infrequent activity, has emerged as a major component of national financial transactions. These equity loans can provide financing not only for further homebuying, but also for a number of other consumer expenditures.

Just as the recent inflationary period left homeowners somewhat richer, it left low-income households in a more difficult housing situation. From 1974 to 1981 the rate of homeownership fell for households with real incomes less than $15,000 (in constant 1981 dollars), but increased for households with incomes in excess of $15,000. As the average income of renters lagged behind that of owner households, the housing condition of renter households deteriorated. From 1974 to 1981, the proportion of all

renter households paying more than 35 percent of their
income for rent increased from 23.1 percent to 32.0 percent, or from 5.8 million to 9.1 million. As should be
expected, the nation's poorest households faced particularly severe payment burdens. In 1981, 6.4 million renter
households with incomes less than $5,000 paid more than 35
percent of their income for rent.

The increased housing problems of the nation's poorest
households deserve attention, but implicit in the forecasts
presented in this study is the assumption that there will
be little or no expansion of housing subsidy payments to
the poorest renter households. The new housing voucher
program would have to be expanded substantially beyond
current levels to make a dent in the problem. It is important to note that all housing programs in operation today
combined provide benefits to less than 4.0 million households. Without an unforeseen increase in the scope of
these programs, the housing payments problem of low- and
moderate-income households will continue to grow in the
years ahead.

Managing the Existing Stock. The 1980s will see new
construction activity begin a downward course that will
last for the next several decades. This does not necessarily imply reduced standards of housing consumption,
depending on how well the nation maintains its existing
housing inventory. According to Joint Center estimates,
even by the year 2000, three of every four U.S. households
will live in a unit that was built before 1980. Local
regulations relating to the maintenance of existing units,
or the conversion of housing to meet the continuing demand
for smaller multi-family units, will have an important
influence on the future cost and condition of U.S. housing
stock. Development of state and local programs to encourage sensible maintenance and reuse of existing housing
is a priority issue for public policy in the 1980s.

Changing Household Composition. In designing policies
for the future, many analysts take the patterns of household formation as given. In translating simple forecasts
of household growth into numerical goals for housing construction, however, they often ignore the fact that public
policy can influence household size and composition.
Rather than attempting to build a housing stock to fit projections of households, public policy can also encourage
the formation of new types of households that make better
use of the existing housing inventory. House-sharing is a

simple example of this approach. By changing zoning laws to permit single individuals to take in boarders, policy makers can help provide housing for single individuals at little additional cost to society. Congregate housing is another example of efforts to house elderly individuals in some way other than the now very common pattern of one person to one unit. In short, public policy must examine programs that encourage the formation of new living arrangements to make better use of the existing housing stock, as well as programs that change the characteristics of the stock to meet demographic change.

Central-City Decline and Rural Revitalization.   While the popular press devoted considerable attention to the back-to-the-city movement, in fact, in the 1970s central cities continued to lose population and employment to the faster-growing areas. Continuation of these mobility patterns poses a number of difficult public policy issues for both the declining central cities and newly growing areas.

Abandonment will continue to plague many of the larger central cities in the 1980s. Although the 1970s witnessed a sharp decline in the removal of units from the inventory, high rates of abandonment continued in the central cities of the largest metropolitan areas of the Northeast and North Central regions. At best, abandonment is an inefficient method for maintaining the supply-and-demand balance in an area. Moreover, in response to the pressures of excess housing supply, the abandonment process frequently goes too far, taking good-quality units with the bad, and destroying the fabric of inner-city neighborhoods.

Somewhat ironically, low-income households are victims of both excess supply and excess demand for housing in their neighborhood. Excess demand can stimulate increased investment in high-cost inner-city housing. This happened in selected inner-city neighborhoods, and the resulting displacement of many low-income households led many communities to ban condominium conversions or other types of investment associated with neighborhood revitalization. At the same time, and often in the same cities, abandonment was continuing to undermine the supply of decent low-cost housing in stable neighborhoods. Public policy efforts to rehabilitate and return abandoned housing to the market often failed, since these programs simply served to exacerbate the problem of excess supply and inadequate demand for inner-city housing. Public policies aimed at inner-city areas must build from a better understanding of the basic factors that influence neighborhood change. Designing such policies will indeed challenge many state and local governments as they seek to compensate for diminished federal involvement in housing issues.

Just as the inner cities must deal with the changing fortunes of individual neighborhoods, so must many communities, especially rural communities, learn to cope with growth. The decentralization of employment and population has restored growth to many areas that have been declining for decades. While at first growth is welcomed, soon these communities begin to see the associated costs. Increased population places strains on the infrastructure and requires careful planning to provide adequate water and sewer facilities. At the same time, many communities must deal with the rapid increase in the school-aged population. This is especially true of the many non-metropolitan areas that are growing primarily as a result of the influx of young families with children.

As these comments suggest, urban decline and rural revitalization are linked and both pose problems of growth management. In urban areas the problem is one of managing decline; in rural areas, one of managing growth. Thus as the schools in one inner-city neighborhood empty, the school-aged population soars in an isolated rural county. Designing national, state, and local policies that enable rural areas to grow wisely and urban areas to decline gracefully is one of the major challenges facing public policy makers in the 1980s.

NOTES

1. U.S. President's Commission on Housing, Report of the President's Commission on Housing (Washington, DC: U.S. Government Printing Office, 1982), p. 4.

BIBLIOGRAPHY

BIBLIOGRAPHY

Advance Mortgage Corporation. U.S. Housing Markets. Detroit, MI: Advance Mortgage Corporation, 1981.

Alonso, William. "The Demographic Factor in Housing for the Balance of This Century" in North American Housing Markets into the Twenty-First Century, edited by Michael A. Goldberg and George W. Gerr. Cambridge, MA: 1983.

Apgar, William C., Jr. "The Changing Utilization of the Housing Inventory: Past Trends and Future Prospects." Working Paper no. 83-1. Cambridge, MA: Joint Center for Urban Studies of MIT and Harvard University, 1983.

---. "The Use of 1980 Census Data for National Policy Research." Paper prepared for U.S. Department of Housing and Urban Development, 1981.

Baker, Kermit. "Housing Affordability." Ph.D. dissertation, Massachusetts Institute of Technology, 1983.

Birch, David L. et al. America's Housing Needs: 1970-1980. Cambridge, MA: Joint Center for Urban Studies of MIT and Harvard University, 1973.

Brown, H. James, Karl Case, and Kermit Baker. "Homeownership and Housing Affordability in the United States, 1963-1983." Cambridge, MA: Joint Center for Urban Studies of MIT and Harvard University, 1983.

Case, Carl. "Land Prices, Housing Prices and Housing Production: Does the Housing Market Work or Doesn't It?" Paper prepared for Joint Center for Urban Studies/ Lincoln Institute of Land Policy Conference, 1982.

Chase Econometrics. RDA Quarterly Forecast Report. Bala Cynwyd, PA: Chase Econometrics, 1983.

Clay, Phillip. "Accessory Apartments." Paper prepared for Lincoln Institute of Land Policy, Cambridge, MA, 1982.

Clephawe, Thomas P. "Outlook for Timber Supply/Demand Through 1990." Paper presented at Workshop on Financing Forestry Investment, Duke University, May 10, 1982.

Data Resources, Inc. "Realities of Long-Run Housing Demand." U.S. Long-term Review. Lexington, MA: Data Resources, Inc., 1981.

---. U.S. Central Data Banks. Lexington, MA: Data Resources, Inc.

Downs, Anthony. Neighborhoods and Urban Development. Washington, DC: The Brookings Institution, 1981.

---. "Search for Space: Rental Housing in the 1980s." Draft report, 1982.

Federal National Mortgage Association. "Housing Finance in the 1980s: Issues and Options." FNMA Symposium, 1981.

Frieden, Bernard J. and Arthur P. Solomon. The Nation's Housing: 1975-1980. Cambridge, MA: Joint Center for Urban Studies of MIT and Harvard University, 1977.

Hack, Gary and Otis Ginoza. "Private and Public Responsibilities in Housing Site Development." Cambridge, MA: Joint Center for Urban Studies of MIT and Harvard University, 1982.

Lowry, Ira S. "Inflation Indexes for Rental Housing." Santa Monica, CA: Rand Corporation, 1982.

---. "Rental Housing in the 1970s: Searching for the Crisis." in Rental Housing: Is There a Crisis? edited by John C. Weicher, Kevin Villani, and Elizabeth Roistacher. Washington, DC: The Urban Institute, 1981.

Marcin, Thomas C. "Outlook for Housing by Type of Unit and Region: 1978 to 2020." USDA Forest Service Research Paper, 1977.

Masnick, George and John Pitkin. The Changing Population of States and Regions. Cambridge, MA: Joint Center for Urban Studies of MIT and Harvard University, 1982.

McGough, Duane. <u>Additions to the Housing Supply by Means</u> <u>Other than New Construction</u>. Washington, DC: U.S. Department of Housing and Urban Development, 1982.

---. "Housing Inventory Losses as a Requirement for New Construction." Paper presented at the Seminar on Housing Forecasting and Programming, U.N. Economic Commission for Europe, 1981.

National Association of Homebuilders. "The Eighties: After a Slow Start, Some Very Good Years." <u>Builder Magazine</u>, January 7, 1980.

National Association of Realtors. "Median Sales Price of Existing Homes for the U.S." Washington, DC: National Association of Realtors, 1968-73.

Phillips, Robyn Swaim. "Explaining the Decline in Real Residential Rents, 1970-1980: The Rental Housing Crisis Reconsidered." Ph.D. dissertation, Harvard University, 1983.

Pitkin, John and George Masnick. "Projections of Housing Consumption in the U.S., 1980 to 2000, by a Cohort Method." <u>Annual Housing Survey Studies</u> no. 9 (1980).

---. "Linking Projections of Households with Housing Con- sumption: An Exploration of Alternative Series." Report prepared for the Office of Policy Development and Research, HUD, 1981.

President's Commission on Housing. <u>Report of the Presi-</u> <u>dent's Commission on Housing</u>. Washington, DC: U.S. Government Printing Office, 1982.

President's Commission on Urban Housing. <u>A Decent Home:</u> <u>Report of the President's Commision on Urban Housing</u>. Washington, DC: U.S. Government Printing Office, 1968.

Regional Data Associates. "Overview of the Models." Bala Cynwyd, PA: Regional Data Associates, Chase Econometrics.

Rosen, Kenneth and Dwight Jaffee. "The Demand for Housing
    and Mortgage Credit: The Mortgage Credit Gap Problem."
    Paper presented at FNMA Symposium on Housing Finance in
    the Eighties, February 1981.

Sternlieb, George and James W. Hughes. "Housing: Past and
    Future." Paper presented at FNMA Symposium on Housing
    Finance in the Eighties, February 1981.

Tuccillo, John. Housing and Investment in an Inflationary
    World: Theory and Evidence. Washington, DC: The Urban
    Institute, 1980.

U.S. Bureau of the Census. Annual Housing Survey: National
    Core File. Washington, DC: U.S. Government Printing
    Office, 1975 and 1980.

---. Annual Housing Survey: National Sample. Washington,
    DC: U.S. Government Printing Office, 1975 and 1980.

---. Annual Housing Survey: national unpublished data,
    1977.

---. Annual Housing Survey tapes. Washington, DC: U.S.
    Government Printing Office, 1975 and 1980.

---. Annual Housing Survey, United States and Regions.
    Part A: General Housing Characteristics. Washington,
    DC: U.S. Department of Housing and Urban Development,
    1973, 1980 and 1982

---. Census of Housing. Vol. 4: Components of Inventory
    Change. (Supplementary reports PC80-S1-2). Washing-
    ton, DC: U.S. Government Printing Office, 1950-70,
    1983.

---. Census of Population: Standard Metropolitan Statis-
    tical Areas and Standard Consolidated Areas. (Supple-
    mentary reports, PC80-S1-5). Washington, DC: U.S.
    Government Printing Office, 1980.

---. Census of Population and Housing, 1970: Estimates of
    Coverage of the Population by Sex, Race, and Age.
    Washington, DC: U.S. Government Printing Office, 1974.

---. Census of Population and Housing, 1970: First Count Summary Tapes. Washington, DC: U.S. Government Printing Office, 1970.

---. Census of Population and Housing, 1980: Public Use Microdata Sample, B Sample. Washington, DC: U.S. Government Printing Office, 1983.

---. Census of Population and Housing, 1980: Provisional Estimates of Social, Economic, and Housing Characteristics. (Supplementary report PHC 80-S1-1). Washington, DC: U.S. Government Printing Office, 1982.

---. Census of Population and Housing, 1980: Summary Tape File 1C. Washington, DC: U.S. Government Printing Office, 1980.

---. Census of Population and Housing: Public Use Sample (1-in-100). Washington, DC: U.S. Government Printing Office, 1960 and 1970.

---. The Coverage of Housing in the 1970 Census. Washington, DC: U.S. Government Printing Office, 1973.

---. Current Population Reports (series P-20, nos. 212, 287, 345, 365, and 366; series P-25, no. 22.) Washington, DC: U.S. Government Printing Office, 1980.

---. Housing Completions (current construction reports, series C-22). Washington, DC: U.S. Government Printing Office, 1970-80.

---. New One-Family Homes Sold and For Sale (current construction reports, series C-25). Washington, DC: U.S. Government Printing Office, 1963-1983.

---. The Post-Enumeration Survey: 1950. Washington, DC: U.S. Government Printing Office, 1960.

---. Survey of Residential Alterations and Repairs (current construction reports, series C-50). Washington, DC: U.S. Government Printing Office, various years.

---. The Value of New Construction Put in Place (current construction reports, series C-30). Washington, DC: U.S. Government Printing Office, various years.

U.S. Congressional Budget Office. Federal Housing Policy:
    Current Programs and Recurrent Issues. Washington, DC:
    U.S. Government Printing Office, 1978.

U.S. Department of Labor, Bureau of Labor Statistics.
    Consumer Price Index: Fuel and Utilities and Mainten-
    ance and Repair. Washington, DC: U.S. Government
    Printing Office, various years.

U.S. Task Force on Housing Costs. Report of the Task Force
    on Housing Costs to the Department of Housing and Urban
    Development. Washington, DC: U.S. Government Printing
    Office, 1978.

Urban Systems Research and Engineering. Economic Impact of
    Environmental Regulations on Housing. Cambridge, MA:
    Urban Systems Research and Engineering, 1981.

Weicher, John, Lorene Yap, and Mary S. Jones. Metropolitan
    Housing Needs for the 1980s. Washington, DC: The Urban
    Institute, 1982.

INDEX

abandonment, 161

absent spouse, 27

adjusting down, 46–48

Advance Mortgage Corporation, 108, 111, 116

affluence, reduced, 49

affordability of housing, 3, 7, 149; problems, 49, 117

age groups, influence on headship rates, 112

age of housing unit, loss rate, 71

age structure, 16, 19–21; differentials in fertility rates, 21

aging of baby-boom generation, 30, 124, 154–55; household gross distribution, 55; interpreting outlook, 154–55; mix of new construction, implications for and, 155 (see also baby-boom generation)

America's Housing Needs: 1970–1980, 2

Annual Housing Survey (AHS), 4, 58, 153; comparison with 1980 census count, 60–62

apartments, 46; conversions to, 6, 54

appreciation, future gains through, 7

baby-boom cohort, 39–41; housing consumption patterns, 37

baby-boom generation, 6, 16; aging of (see aging of

baby-boom generation); economic recession effect on, 141; housing market prediction, 105; maturing of, 11; never married group, 19; prime home buying stages, 7

baby-bust generation, 16; maturing of, 124; uniform distribution, 21

back-to-the-city movement, 161

births: decline in 1960s, 21; effects on household formation, 111

Brookings Institute, 108

capital gains, tax-free, 86

Census of Population and Housing (1980), 4

central-city decline, 161–62

central-city housing stock, gentrification and rehabilitation of, 80

Changing Population of States and Regions, The, 4

child-oriented life styles, 13

CINCH statistics (1980) (see Components of Inventory Change [CINCH] Report [1980])

cohort analysis, 35

cohort approach, housing consumption, 36–37

Components of Inventory Change (CINCH) Report (1980), 62, 64

condominiums, 49, 152; affordability, 8; conversions to, 6, 54; homeownership costs and, 86; young renters, 50

congregate housing, 161

171

ABOUT THE AUTHORS

WILLIAM C. APGAR, JR. is Associate Professor of City and Regional Planning at the John F. Kennedy School of Government, Harvard University, Cambridge, MA. He is Research Director of the Housing Futures Project at the Joint Center for Housing Studies of MIT and Harvard University.

Dr. Apgar has published several books and articles. Among his publications are Housing and Neighborhood Dynamics: A Simulation Study with John F. Kain (Cambridge, MA: Harvard University Press, 1985) and Property Taxes, Housing and the Cities with George E. Peterson, Arthur P. Solomon, and Hadi Madjid, (Lexington, MA: D.C. Heath, 1973).

Dr. Apgar holds a B.A. from Williams College and a Ph.D. from Harvard University.

H. JAMES BROWN is Professor of City and Regional Planning at John F. Kennedy School of Government, Harvard University, Cambridge, MA. He is also Director of the State, Local, and Intergovernmental Center and the MIT/Harvard Joint Center for Housing Studies, Harvard University, and Research Associate at the National Bureau of Economic Research.

Dr. Brown has published numerous books, reports, and papers. Among his works are "Homeownership and Housing Affordability in the United States, 1963–1984" (Joint Center for Housing Studies, 1985) and "Landownership and Market Dynamics at Urban Periphery: Implications for Land Policy Design and Implementation," in World Congress on Land Policy, 1980 (Lexington, MA: Lexington Press, 1982).

Dr. Brown received a B.A. from Ohio Wesleyan University and a Ph.D. from Indiana University.

GEORGE S. MASNICK is Research Associate at the MIT/Harvard Joint Center for Housing Studies, Cambridge, MA. He is President of Analysis and Forecasting, Inc., Cambridge, MA, and Adjunct Lecturer in Public Policy at the John F. Kennedy School of Government, Harvard University.

Dr. Masnick's several publications include <u>The Nation's Families, 1960-1990</u> with Mary Jo Bane, et al (Boston, MA: Auburn House, 1980) and <u>Regional Diversity: Growth in the U.S., 1960-1990</u>, with Gregory Jackson and others (Boston, MA: Auburn House, 1981).

Dr. Masnick has a B.A. from Cornell University, an M.A. from Cornell University, and a Ph.D. from Brown University.

JOHN PITKIN has published widely in the field of urban studies. Among his publications are "Projections of Housing Consumption in the U.S., 1980 to 2000, by a Cohort Method," with George Masnick (U.S. Department of Housing and Urban Development, Annual Housing Survey Study, No. 9, Washington, 1980) and <u>Regional Diversity: Growth in the U.S., 1960-1990</u>, with Gregory Jackson, George Masnick, Roger Bolton, and Susan Bartlett (Boston, MA: Auburn House, 1981).

Mr. Pitkin received a B.A. from Columbia University, attended graduate school at Oxford University and the University of Helsinki.